HOOVER INSTITUTE STUDIES

Series B: Elite Studies, No. 8   July 1952

KUOMINTANG AND CHINESE COMMUNIST ELITES

by Robert C. North

with the collaboration of
Ithiel de Sola Pool

Introduction by John K. Fairbank

The Hoover Institute and Library
on War, Revolution, and Peace
Stanford University

STANFORD UNIVERSITY PRESS

THE HOOVER INSTITUTE STUDIES

This series of studies undertakes to describe the world revolution of our time and its consequences for world politics and national policy. These studies were conducted by the Hoover Institute and Library on War, Revolution, and Peace as part of its research project on Revolution and the Development of International Relations (RADIR Project).

The studies and their publication were made possible by funds granted by Carnegie Corporation of New York. That Corporation is not, however, the author, owner, publisher, or proprietor of this publication, and it is not to be understood as approving by virtue of its grant any of the statements made or views expressed therein.

STANFORD UNIVERSITY PRESS
STANFORD, CALIFORNIA

Copyright 1952 by the Board of Trustees
of the Leland Stanford Junior University

Printed in the United States of America
by Stanford University Press

First printing, August 1952
Second printing, June 1953
Third printing, October 1954

Library of Congress Catalog Card Number: 52-3689

PREFACE

The biographical material for this study has been gathered from sources which differ greatly in their reliability. Information concerning leaders of the Empire was drawn from Arthur Hummel, ed., Eminent Chinese of the Ch'ing Period (1644–1912), U.S. Library of Congress, Washington (1943–44), a standard work. Information concerning Kuomintang leaders was extracted from the third and fifth editions of Who's Who in China, from the China Year Book, 1929–30, from the Chinese Handbook, 1945, and from the private files of observers with long years of residence in China. A portion of the material on Kuomintang clique affiliation comes from Biographies of Kuomintang Leaders, mimeographed by the Committee on International and Regional Studies, Harvard University, February 1948. This volume is a translation of materials used by Chinese Communist intelligence agencies which, for all their bias, would presumably take some care in compiling classified information about their opponents. The fact remains, however, that the validity of this source is open to question, and allowances for possible error should therefore be made in considering quantifications of Kuomintang clique affiliations.

In gathering material concerning Chinese Communist leaders, the author sought sources which, in one fashion or another, had been close to the Chinese Communist movement. Considerable bodies of vital statistics were gleaned from the books of Nym Wales and Edgar Snow, both of whom have interviewed numbers of Chinese Communist leaders, taking down biographical notes. The bulk of material, however, came from individual informants who donated much of their valuable time and information in order to fill out the author's questionnaires. For their co-operation in tabulating Communist or Kuomintang biographical material from their files, the author is indebted to a large number of persons including Michael Lindsay, John Bottorff, John W. Powell, Dr. George E. Taylor, Maurice Votaw, and Professor E. H. Cressy.

A very special debt is owed Miss Rosemary Riley, who, laboring long hours over card files and columns of statistics, displayed a remarkable genius for ferreting out the author's errors. Conrad Brandt, Dr. John K. Fairbank, Dr. Martin Wilbur, Dr. Karl A. Wittfogel, and Dr. Mary Wright read the manuscript and offered a large number of valuable criticisms and suggestions. The author is further indebted to Dr. Harold H. Fisher, Dr. C. Easton Rothwell, and Dr. Daniel Lerner for their constant aid and support, and to Howard Boorman and Mrs. Anna B. Wheeler for their warm encouragement.

By far the greater share of credit for the quantitative findings belongs with Ithiel deSola Pool, who, collaborating on chapter iv, brought order out of a statistical chaos and traced trends which might have been missed by other eyes. For chapter iv, then, Dr. Pool shares both credit and responsibility, but for all errors of omission and commission in the rest of the paper, this author is solely responsible.

Hoover Institute and Library   Robert C. North
on War, Revolution, and Peace

July 1, 1952

iii

18875

INTRODUCTION

The party organizations of the Kuomintang and the Chinese Communists, so vividly analyzed by Robert North in this monograph, have both represented attempts at the creation and use of political power in the modern Chinese state. The history and structure of these two party dictatorships are of peculiar and melancholy interest to American readers, for it has been plain for thirty years past that our type of Anglo-Saxon parliamentary democracy has not been able to provide the model for successful political organization in China. It is surely no accident of history that Sun Yat-sen's Kuomintang reorganized in 1923, and the Chinese Communist Party founded in 1921, both Leninist-type organizations, have been the only real contenders for power in China since that time. We are here confronted with a basic inadaptability of the Western European—American political system when applied to the agrarian-bureaucratic Chinese state.

Except in this one respect of the organization of political power, we may well claim that the West has fathered the Chinese revolution. No matter what judgment we render upon the rights and wrongs of the imperialist epoch, we cannot deny that until very recently the modern century of Chinese history has received its preponderant foreign influence from the West. Even the important and little-studied influence of Japan upon modern China was in part a reflection of the Western impact upon Japan. The Western commerce, arms, and law which begat the treaty ports, the Western missionary education which undermined Confucianism, the return of Western-trained Chinese who stood for individualism, and the influx of Western ideas on all levels have contributed to this revolutionary process. Western contact has been subversive of the old order in China and has inspired great new developments—not least, the rise of nationalism. Yet in all this long and manifold process of intercultural contact, the non-Communist West has not given China's leaders the secret of how to organize a modern political process.

Sun Yat-sen was one of the first to face this basic problem. As early as 1905 he developed a formula which has been echoed ever since—the formula of political tutelage under a monolithic party which would be the self-appointed guardian of the Chinese people's political development. As Mr. North points out, this paternalistic conception sprang directly from China's long tradition of rule by sage-emperors who exercised a nominally benevolent despotism. Having from time immemorial been governed by an elite, the masses of the Chinese peasantry could work their way into democracy only by stages. For all his eclecticism and equivocation, Dr. Sun was the first political leader to recognize this fact. Unfortunately he could not clearly foresee that political tutelage by a self-appointed elite in preparation for popular democracy could hardly escape the modern menace of totalitarian manipulation.

The question whether modern China could in fact have avoided the growth of an increasingly totalitarian party dictatorship is one that deserves our

closest study. Who shall say that the Chinese people must now for the fore-
seeable future remain in bondage to a statist philosophy? Can we be sure
that the Chinese Communist rise to power has been "inevitable"? A closer
view of China's modern history may give us doubts: if the Japanese invasion of the 1930's had not destroyed the Western-oriented sector of modern
Chinese life, might not the Nanking government have been able, even if
belatedly, to realize Sun's vision and bring the people more fully into the
government? May we not conclude, indeed, that the Communist Party's rise
to power in the fifteen years since its low point of 1935 –36 (after the
Long March), has in fact been a product of special and temporary circumstances— such as the sudden, enforced awakening of the sentiment of nationalism among a populace still inured to elitist forms of leadership?

Mr. North's analysis of the six Central Executive Committees selected
by the Kuomintang between 1924 and 1945 shows the steady gravitation of
power into the hands of Chiang Kai-shek, as the head and forefront of the
CC or "organization" group within the party. Yet this intraparty process
went on within the larger context of the Japanese invasion and China's
eventual war of resistance, during which the Kuomintang government became almost steadily weaker and less capable of fulfilling its role of political tutelage over the Chinese people. Here we see, certainly, a vicious
circle—the concentration of personal power within the regime pari passu
with its loss of power within the state. It is safe to say that Chiang Kai-shek's
control of his regime has never been greater than now on Formosa in its
period of greatest impotence.

Surely this is more than a matter of personality—the political institutions of the Chinese state, it may be suggested, have provided the setting
both for Chiang's rise as a leader of the new nationalism and for his fall
as a holder of power which had become essentially personal. First, the
rise of the Kuomintang to power in the 1920's represented a new ascendancy
of "nationalism" as the sanction for authority. This triumphed easily over
the ancient Confucian principle of personal rule through wang-tao (the
"Kingly way") which various war lords had tried to revive and which the
Japanese anachronistically promoted in the 1930's in Manchuria and North
China. Second, however, the rise of the Communists to power in the 1940's
must be attributed in large part to their exploitation of this new Chinese
nationalism in a more developed form. They made it a movement which
aimed not only at the unity, independence, and glory of the "Chinese nation"
but also at the "liberation," salvation, and rejuvenation of the "Chinese
people." Their application of Marxism-Leninism to China was able to use
social forces for political purposes more broadly and deeply than Sun or
Chiang had done. This was because the doctrines of Maoism promised a
more adequate solution of China's great national problems, which basically
were economic and social rather than merely political in nature. Thus the
sanction for the exercise of authority during this modern growth of nationalism has come to reside somewhat less in personal political conduct and
somewhat more in socio-economic principles and programs. In the intra-

party conflicts which this monograph surveys the two parties are distin-
guished by the personal rivalries among the KMT "ins" in contrast with
the doctrinal struggles among the CCP "outs." In this context Chiang's
fall may be attributed to his lack of an adequate doctrine and effective program, while the Communists' chief danger today lies in a recrudescence
of personal government under their aegis.

These considerations lend significance to the study of the social origins
of the KMT and CCP leaders, between whom the authors find a high degree
of similarity in class background and social status, early training, age
level, and channels of advancement. One of their many arresting observa-
tions is that China's modern political elite seems to have suffered a "downward social mobility"; it has been a "socially declining and discomfited
elite," steadily worse off in personal circumstances. With this process
has been connected the rise of men of actual peasant origin, in large part
through army channels.

Given the similarities of these two groups of "rootless professional
politicians," it is highly instructive to trace, as is done below, the process of polarization by which the KMT became a city-based, merchant-
minded, South and East China congeries of conservatives while the CCP
in the hinterland became a more village-based, ideologically minded
organization of revolutionists centered in the North and Northwest. This
split between a city and a country orientation widened as time went on,
while other factors of divergence also continued to operate — among them,
the CCP capacity to keep their military leadership under the strict ideological control of the party line while the KMT under Chiang continued the
traditional juggling act, to keep regional war lords or military factions
balanced in a framework of personal politics which was practically devoid
of ideology.

Between the two parties here contrasted, the one shuffling off as the
other comes on, the greatest difference would seem to lie in the use of
ideology as a factor in the exercise of political control over the Chinese
people. It is here that we of the non-Communist West entered the Chinese
scene, for our influence dissolved and discredited Confucianism within three
generations. Yet it is on this score again that we have now been, for the
moment, cast out of Chinese life. By the same token it is primarily through
understanding the mind of modern China that we may expect eventually to
construct a new and better relationship across the Pacific.

Here lies one value of this study, in the way it helps us assimilate the
new Communist elite into our accepted picture of the Chinese scene. Given
the unfortunate bifurcation, in American scholarship of the interwar
decades, between the specialists on China and the specialists on communism,
we stand in great need of the combined view which Mr. North provides.

John K. Fairbank

TABLE OF CONTENTS

I. THE COLLAPSE OF THE IMPERIAL ELITE

Since the fall of the Manchu Empire in 1911, the Chinese Revolution has seen the development of two highly organized elite bodies — the Kuomintang and the Chinese Communist Party — which have interacted in such a complicated fashion that it is almost impossible to isolate the growth and decay of one from the development of the other.

Each emerged from the political, social, and economic chaos which came with the impact of Western culture upon Chinese society and with the breakdown of the Ch'ing dynasty. Each was a blend of indigenous impulse and foreign political theory and organization. Each co-operated with the other when its interests required. Each sought the other's annihilation once political circumstances changed.

Thus, within the course of a single lifetime, early members of the Kuomintang have developed from a counterelite (under the Empire) to a ruling elite; have co-operated with and have sought to destroy the Chinese Communists; have enjoyed enormous prestige and power; have suffered military defeats; and have now been pushed from the mainland of China. During the space of an even shorter lifetime, the Communists have grown from a few disorganized left-wing intellectual discussion groups into a thoroughly organized and tightly disciplined conspiratorial organization; have allied themselves with and have sought to destroy the Kuomintang; have been forced underground and nearly exterminated; have risen again and have now become the de facto rulers of China.

The revolutionary pattern, as developed first by the Kuomintang and later by the Communists, displayed a number of distinctive features. To a notable extent, both leadership elites were composed of culturally alienated intellectuals — men and women of well-to-do families who had removed themselves from the orthodox stream of their society's traditional culture. In both, this peculiar trend resulted from powerful foreign influences on the economy of China and on its intellectual leaders. In both cases, most members of this displaced intellectual elite rose to revolutionary power by devoting their lives to political organization and action and by using their inherited high social status to change the directions of Chinese cultural trends.

This new elite scheme presented a sharp contrast to the imperial pattern of the Ch'ing dynasty. The political leadership of the Chinese Empire functioned within a system which has been described as "an autocracy superimposed upon a democracy." The Emperor was the balance between heaven and earth, but in return for his divine right to rule, he assumed a large responsibility for the maintenance of order, peace, and prosperity within his realm. If he should fail in this, it was assumed that his subjects would rebel against him.

Yet the Emperor ruled, an absolute and legally unlimited monarch, with

1

various of the imperial clan clustered about him. Directly below him in
the administrative hierarchy came the Grand Council and the Grand Secretariat, and below these came six (eventually increased to twelve) departments or boards roughly comparable to ministries. Under the central government came the provincial administrations headed in each case by a
governor-general (viceroy) and/or a governor. In addition to these officials,
the Ch'ing dynasty established in eleven provinces the post of Tartar-gen-
eral, who ranked "with, but before" the viceroy.

Each province was divided into smaller units designated as tao or cir-
cuits over which an intendant presided. Each tao was made up of fu (over-
seen by a prefect), and the fu, in turn, were subdivided into departments
(under departmental magistrates) and hsien (under magistrates). These
officials secured their appointments from above, all commissions being
issued by the Emperor. But within the departments and hsien were also
town and village officials who secured their mandates from popular support.

Throughout the whole governmental system, the securing of public office depended to a considerable extent upon the possession of one of three
literary degrees—hsiu ts'ai, chü jen, and chin shih.

Examinations for the hsiu ts'ai were held in prefectural cities for students who had first been screened by tests given by the magistrates in their
hsien (districts). Provincial examinations for the chü jen were usually held
triennially in the autumn at the various provincial capitals. Normally, out
of some ten to twelve thousand competitors, in each province, only about
three hundred were passed. [1]

Theoretically, these examinations, which anyone, with few exceptions,
was privileged to take, served as the gateways to public life, but how the
system actually functioned is still a subject for investigation. Writing in
1938, Dr. Karl A. Wittfogel came to the tentative conclusion that whereas
some "fresh blood" from lower strata of society may have been absorbed
through the examination system, the prevailing tendency was for the ruling
elite to reproduce itself socially by recruiting from its own ranks. Wittfogel's material, drawn largely from the Dynastic Histories, included two
dynasties, Han (206 B.C. —A.D. 22) and Chin (265 —420), falling prior to
the establishment of the examination system, together with the T'ang (618 —
906), Sung (906 —1279), Yuan (1280 —1368), and Ming (1368 —1644) eras. [2]
In recent years, this data has been found to contrast with material gathered
by Dr. Edward A. Kracke, Jr. , from early lists of civil service examination graduates. [3]

On the evidence of two lists (A.D. 1148 and 1256), a majority of candidates who passed the examinations seem to have emerged from nonofficial
families. It is Dr. Kracke's conclusion, then, that although the topmost
elite of Chinese officialdom, as represented by biographies in the Dynastic
Histories, was recruited, for the most part, from official families, the
entire body of candidates passing through the examination system was notably more representative of lower strata of Chinese society.

An examination of twenty-three late nineteenth-century and early twenti-eth-century Empire careers, drawn for illustrative purposes from a de-finitive biographical source,[4] reveals a number of diverse patterns.

TABLE I. STATISTICS ON THE LIVES OF TWENTY-THREE LEADERS OF THE CH'ING DYNASTY BETWEEN 1890 AND 1911

Background	Number
Scholar-official family	7
Minor government official (father)	3
Imperial family (father)	3
Merchant (father)	2
Army officer (father)	1
Peasant (father)	1
Outlaw	1
Don't know	5

Prerequisite for office	
Chin Shih degree	8
Chü Jen degree	2
Hsiu Ts'ai degree	1

Among those who did not pass through the examination system:

Purchase	2
Royal birth	3
Knowledge of English language	1
Military service (officer)	2
Military service (promotion from ranks)	1
Royal concubine	1
Royal eunuch	1
Private education	1

Of this illustrative (but not necessarily statistically representative) sample, the large majority came from official families. Indeed, only four out of the eighteen on whom we have information had fathers in private oc-cupations. A very thin stratum of the millions of Chinese families actually constituted the ruling elite despite the nominally democratic character of the examination system. The father of only one of the leaders came from among the hundreds of millions of peasants. The much smaller merchant class contributed two sons to our sample of the imperial elite, which was not disproportionate to their numbers in the population but contrasts with

the many sons of officials. The business classes had not yet gained easy
access to the centers of governmental prestige, although education provided a possible portal for men of business background. [5]

Of the twenty-three leaders not quite half entered their careers through
the portals of the examination system. Twelve, however, managed to reach
office through other channels. In general the scholars, officials, and merchants, the counterparts of the middle classes in the West, sent their sons
through the regular examination process more often than did the others.
Those sons who entered public careers without the advantage of imperial ancestry or who struggled into public careers from less-favored
backgrounds were the ones who made their way into public office through
irregular channels.

Of the seven sons of scholar-officials, five took examinations.

Of the three sons of minor officials, two took examinations.

Of the two sons of merchants, both took examinations.

The remaining two leaders who entered public office through the examination system are among those whose fathers' occupations we do not know.
Thus the examination system was part of a pattern by which persons from
scholar-official-merchant backgrounds entered public life. How the other
half of our sample entered reveals some alternative patterns.

Of the two sons of scholar-officials who did not take examinations, one
had studied under a private tutor and one purchased his first position. The
one leader whose father was a minor government official and who did not
take examinations was a girl who acquired her position by becoming a royal
concubine— and eventually Empress Dowager of China.

Among members of the Imperial family, I-huan, the seventh son of the
Kuang-hsü emperor by a concubine, was created a prince of the second
degree during his tenth year and lieutenant general of the banner during his
twenty-first year; his elder brother, I-hsin, was made Grand Councillor
at the age of twenty; and the Kuang-hsu emperor, the second son of I-huan,
was adopted during his childhood by the Empress Dowager in violation of
the laws of succession and ascended the throne at the age of four years.

A brigadier general's son helped to organize the first army corps in
China to be equipped with modern arms and to be drilled in the Western
manner. At twenty-eight the son made brigade rank, and two years later he
was promoted to the grade of lieutenant general. Concurrently he held civilian positions and rose to a Grand Secretaryship.

The son of a peasant entered a missionary school, then studied in Macao,
Hong Kong, and Monson Academy in Massachusetts, and eventually gradu-
ated from Yale. Later his knowledge of English yielded him a position in the
Imperial Customs Service and started him on a career that led into diplo-
macy.

Feng Tzu-ts'ai, brought up as an outlaw, was head of a band by the time
he reached his early thirties. Later he entered the Imperial Army and won
rapid promotions.

One man of influence— Li Lien-ying, a eunuch— scarcely fits into any

conventional classification. Born of "humble parents," he was apprenticed
to a cobbler at an early age. He appears to have had no schooling, no money
to buy rank, and no military power or experience, but through extreme
self-sacrifice—suffered during his sixteenth year—he was able to enter
the Imperial Service, whereupon, by the crafty use of remaining talents,
he in time became one of the most powerful persons in the Empire.

The Western Impact

By the middle of the nineteenth century the whole body of Empire leadership (of which these individuals were but a small segment) were struggling
to meet the threat of foreign conquest.

Invasion, of course, was nothing new to the Chinese people. But twenti-
eth-century conquest was something of a different sort, for the modern
invader won his ground less by force of arms than by technology and Western finance; the great campaigns were not military expeditions but con-
struction jobs; and the columns that began pushing their way across China
were railroads rather than regiments of infantry.

Chinese leaders were discovering themselves to be nearly helpless
against this onslaught. The country had no effective weapons—no powerful
finance, no modern technology—for resisting, nor could they be obtained
except from foreign sources.

During the nineteenth-century, various European states had induced the
Manchu Empire to open a number of ports to foreign trade, and then, with
this foothold, they had pushed inland, leasing, building railroads, buying
up concessions, and lending money. The dilemma was inescapable, for if
China were to build its economic defenses, it needed both money and railroads, but each new acquisition of this sort brought a deeper entrenchment
of foreign influence. Among the results were further indebtedness and
balances of trade unfavorable to China.

China's leadership could not agree upon proper measures. During the
nineteenth century, sincere and able efforts had been made to adjust the
governmental structure for coping not only with the direct foreign impact
but also with the internal dislocations that soon resulted from the invasion
of an alien culture. But the framework and machinery and functions of the
Empire remained inadequate.

There was undoubtedly a complex variety of reasons for this inadequacy.
This most recent invasion—in contrast to earlier ones—depended upon a
more complex system of commercial and mechanical techniques than
Chinese culture had so far produced. Its transportation system was more
highly developed than those of previous invasions and of China itself. Its
warfare was more highly mechanized and mobilized. Its trade lines, its
communications, its whole cultural pattern had spread out over continents
and seas and had, in a sense, nearly surrounded China before the invasion
began.

In addition, there were uncommon weaknesses in the Imperial structure

itself. The ruling Manchu dynasty, which was still not completely assimi-
lated, was perhaps less adaptable, less resilient, and less sensitive to
moods of the Chinese people than a thoroughly indigenous dynasty might
have been. Corruption had been spreading within the hierarchy. The
Empress Dowager was self-willed, stubborn, and intolerant of opposition
on the part of her subordinates.

Individual leaders ranged themselves according to their attitudes toward
the foreign impact. Some, like the Empress Dowager, hoped to resist
through rigid preservation of the structure as it was; others wanted to
modify structure, machinery, and functions to cope with foreign influences
and new conditions; and still others saw no solution short of tearing down
the old framework and rebuilding according to Western models.

The Communist Influence

Such was the background against which liberal and conservative elements
struggled for influence during the last two decades of Manchu rule and
from which both the Kuomintang and Chinese Communist leaderships gradually emerged. But it was Russian communism that godfathered both new
parties.

Prior to 1924 Dr. Sun Yat-sen's Kuomintang remained weak, disorganized, and floundering. Comprising a peculiar mixture of idealistic intellectuals and treaty port merchants, the movement had no army or unified
party structure. In his later years Dr. Sun was in poor health; rank-and-
file membership was scattered; and party headquarters in Canton depended
upon the whimsical good will of local war lords for its security.[6]

Leaders of world communism became interested in the Kuomintang when
they convinced themselves that this party, which stressed national equality
and unity as its main reason for being, could be turned to Communist purposes. In 1920 the Second Congress of the Communist International developed a strategy for harnessing Asian revolutions that were already under
way and for bringing them to bear against the forces of world capitalism.
In this plan, however, there were two mutually contradictory concepts
which plagued Bolshevik leaders through early phases of Chinese Communist
history and which were not satisfactorily resolved until the rise of Mao
Tse-tung to leadership.

At the Second Congress, M. N. Roy, an Indian delegate who later separated himself from the Communist movement, stressed the belief that Western capitalism was drawing its chief strength from colonial possessions and
dependencies. Without this control of raw materials and markets, he said,
the capitalist powers of the world could not maintain their existence. "Super-
profit gained in the colonies," he said, "is the mainstay of modern capitalism, and so long as the latter is not deprived of this source of super-profit,
it will not be easy for the European working class to overthrow the capitalist
order."[7]

Lenin accepted this principle, maintaining that it was implicit in his own
earlier writings, but he criticized the emphasis Roy placed on class con-

flict in Asia. Roy, he felt, went too far in declaring that the destiny of the West would depend exclusively upon the development and strength of peasant and working-class revolts in Asian countries. On the contrary, Lenin considered it necessary for all Communist parties to enlarge their influence by rendering assistance to existing "bourgeois-democratic liberation movements" in economically backward areas where, he said, working-class revolutions were not as yet sufficiently matured to be effective.

In seeking to resolve this contradiction between class conflict and the concept of co-operation with nationalist revolutions, the Second Congress accepted both, in what amounted to a policy of co-operation combined with opposition. While extending support to middle-class nationalist movements such as the Kuomintang, Communist leaders were expected to arouse and organize the working masses and to penetrate and gain leadership over the revolutionary groups they were aiding.

The reasoning behind this strategy was expressed by a Chinese Communist delegate to the Fourth Congress of the Communist International in 1922:

> If we do not join this party [the Kuomintang] we shall remain isolated and we shall preach a communism which consists of a great and noble ideal, but one which the masses do not follow. The masses certainly would follow the bourgeois party, and this party would use the masses for its purposes. If we join the party, we shall be able to show the masses that we too are for a revolutionary democracy, but that for us revolutionary democracy is only a means to an end. Furthermore, we shall be able to point out that although we are for this distant goal, we nevertheless do not forget the daily needs of the masses. We shall be able to gather the masses around us and split the Kuomintang party. [8]

Bolshevik success in regard to co-operation with the Kuomintang was not immediate, but in January 1923 Adolph Joffe, the Soviet Ambassador in Peking, met Sun in Shanghai and concluded an agreement which became the basis for closer relations before the year was out. During the late summer, Michael Borodin arrived in Canton as adviser to Dr. Sun, and a complete reorganization of the Kuomintang was undertaken.

In China the tradition of professional military and political classes was strong, but under Russian influence the Kuomintang and the Chinese Communist parties both developed special kinds of military and political elites. These were leadership groups which devoted themselves to military service and to political organization and administration with special party frameworks. A vast majority of Kuomintang and Chinese Communist leaders have risen to power and influence through these specialized activities.

There are other initial similarities between Kuomintang and Chinese Communist elites. Both emerged from the political, social, and economic chaos which came with the impact of Western culture upon Chinese society and with the breakdown of the Ch'ing dynasty. Both came from similar socio-economic groups—from landlord, scholar, or bureaucratic families, from merchant or moneylender circles, or from the newly developed capitalist class of large cities along the coast.

In the early stages of their developments, both elites tended to receive their educations in Japan, Europe, or the United States. In the beginning, both sought to break away from the main flow of traditional Chinese culture and practice, although, with the passage of time, the Kuomintang, at best, moved closer to the older current. Both bodies developed schisms and conducted purges, but neither tended to take drastic action against its own disobedients. Both relied heavily on military force.

The divergencies between the two elites are equally noteworthy. The Kuomintang, which began as a Western-oriented, middle-class revolutionary movement with undisciplined organization and ill-defined goals, became increasingly radical with the introduction of Russian influence—but only up to the point where revolution threatened the security of members springing from the landowning and merchant classes. At that contingency the Kuomintang leadership, seeking to preserve both power and property, swung over into a course—increasingly militaristic and counterrevolutionary—which severed their contact with, and brought them into opposition to, a large section of the population, especially the peasantry. The Communists, although shifting their strategy, never abandoned their central plan for capturing the Chinese revolution and using it for their own special purposes.

In moving closer to the flow of traditional Chinese culture, the Kuomintang, which had emerged as an embodiment of Chinese nationalism, tried to adapt a kind of neo-Confucianism to problems of the twentieth century. The Chinese Communists, on the other hand, took the concepts of nationalism, democracy, and the people's livelihood which Sun Yet-sen and his followers had developed, set them in a Marxist-Leninist framework, and gave them a totally new meaning.

Although Kuomintang organization and principles of party discipline were superficially similar to those of the Chinese Communists, the actual functioning of the two parties was different. Chiang Kai-shek rose to power largely through military alliances, police force, quickly executed coups, and the weaving of antagonistic factions—to which he himself did not belong—into an interlacing political system. The Communists succeeded through skillful adaptation of Leninist strategy and tactics to Chinese conditions. Mao and his followers, while championing the cause of the peasant, made what use they could of calculated alliances with the Kuomintang. Supporting Chiang when Chiang was useful, they trained peasant armies to turn against him when the proper moment came. Chiang, though fully aware of Communist purposes, never devised an effective counterprogram nor succeeded in eradicating the Kuomintang's inefficiency, corruption, and complacency, which Communist leadership continually exploited.

II. THE DEVELOPMENT OF THE KUOMINTANG LEADERSHIP

Since 1924 there have been six National Congresses of the KMT Party and six Central Executive Committees. We take the members of these CEC as our sample of the leadership of the Kuomintang. Through the years the relative power of these bodies has varied, but their structure and their position within the Party framework has remained essentially as fixed by Borodin and Sun Yat-sen.

When Borodin reached China in the latter part of 1923, he found Sun Yat-sen's revolutionary movement disunited and floundering. Among seamen of the port cities, among coolies, among workers in British and Japanese textile factories, among students and intellectuals, there existed a powerful revolutionary potential. But Sun and his Kuomintang had not yet been able to harness this dynamic nor to drive it in any consistent direction.

It was clear that the Kuomintang needed advice, material aid, and disciplined leadership— all of which Borodin was in a position to offer.

Sun Yat-sen was not unaware of Kuomintang weaknesses, and consequently Borodin found the Chinese leader in a receptive frame of mind. For a number of years Sun had been trying to secure European and American aid for the support of a Republic of China, but without tangible result. Now, through Borodin, the Soviet Union was offering arms, ammunition, and technical advice— the very support that Sun had felt in need of.

The First Central Executive Committee

Under Borodin's supervision the Kuomintang was rebuilt along the Communist Party pattern, with a series of organizational units pyramiding upward through subdistrict, district, and provincial levels to an annual National Congress, designed as the final authority on both Party and governmental policy, and a Central Executive Committee to direct Party affairs between meetings of the Congress.

In theory, at least, this system (like that of Communist parties) was tied together by democratic centralism. The usual interpretation of this principle is that free discussion must be allowed within all party organs until the moment a decision has been reached, at which point unconditional obedience is required of all members regardless of private disagreement. In other terms, party membership elected authorities to higher echelons, either directly or through intervening congresses, whereupon such authorities were endowed with powers of command and the right to be obeyed. Theoretically, then, the mandate of power flowed upward through the party pyramid, while control fanned downward. In practice, it has usually come about under democratic centralism that whatever authorities control the central organization of a party actually control the party. In this respect the Kuomintang has not proved itself an exception.

Within the Kuomintang there have been four structural levels pyramiding upward from Ch'ü through Hsien, Provincial, and Central Organizations.

Each of these tiers has maintained executive and supervising committees. These are elected at the Ch'ü level by Party members, but in higher echelons they are elected by congresses of Party delegates who, in turn, are elected by the congress of a lower level. Each level has maintained a Party secretary and a series of commissions and departments appointed by and responsible to the appropriate executive committee. Among these various units, the Organizational Department, controlling the organization of Party branches beneath it, has enjoyed exceptional power. [9]

The Kuomintang Constitution (Art. 29) left to the discretion of the Central Executive Committee the actual drafting of regulations concerning the organization of the National Congress, the election of delegates, and the appointment of representatives to the Convention. Thereupon, on the grounds that only the province of Kwangtung (i.e. the area around Canton), was under Kuomintang jurisdiction at the time of the First and Second Congresses in 1924 and 1926, the Central Executive Committee felt justified in instituting the practice of designating delegates from relatively inaccessible areas, a circumvention of democratic process which established something of a precedent and which subsequently evoked considerable criticism from opponents of Kuomintang policy. [10]

The duties of the National Congress included the adoption and approving of National Government reports, the revision of the Party platform and Constitution, the formulation of new policies and programs for the National Government, and the election of members to the Central Executive and Central Supervisory Committees. Between sessions of the National Congress, the Central Executive Committee constituted the highest authority of the Party (Art. 10). To it was entrusted the political authority of the National Government whenever the National Kuomintang Congress was not in session.

It was stipulated that the Central Executive Committee should hold plenary sessions at least once each six months and should elect a Standing Committee of five to nine members to transact business between plenary sessions of the parent organization. Directly beneath the Standing Committee of the Central Executive Committee were ranged a secretariat, an organizational department, a publicity department, a training department, a bureau for statistics, and four special committees dealing with finance, the affairs of overseas Chinese, the drafting of documents, and the compilation of Party history. [11]

In theory, all political sanction was supposed to flow from the bottom of the Party pyramid toward the top. However, the Party constitution (Art. 21), designated Dr. Sun as President of the Party throughout his lifetime, and stated that "the members should follow the direction of the President and work for the advancement of the Party" (Art. 22); that the President should have the power to disapprove resolutions of the Party Congress (Art. 25), and that his voice should be the decisive one in the Central Executive Committee (Art. 26). Sun could, if he chose, exercise complete dictatorial authority over both Party and Government. As long as Dr. Sun lived there was a degree of cohesion within Kuomintang membership, but after his death existing factions began a struggle for power which continued for more than a decade. In a rough fashion these cliques formed themselves initially into three main groups: the extreme right, or Western Hills faction, which opposed the Communist alliance from the very beginning; a middle group which formed itself around Chiang Kai-shek; and a leftwing under the leadership of Wang Ching-wei, Eugene Chen, Mme. Sun Yat-sen, and others.[12]

From the time of its election, the First Central Executive Committee of the Kuomintang suffered spasms of internal strife, but it was not until Dr. Sun's death on March 12, 1925, that these conflicts became severe enough to threaten the Party's existence. During Dr. Sun's final illness, Kuomintang leaders were in almost continual session, in various parts of China, in an effort to decide upon a new leadership. There was dissension in all sections of the Party, but those most bitterly opposed to the Communist alliance, known later as the Western Hills group, were the only ones to take precipitate action. These went so far as to form a separate club with headquarters at 44 Route Vallon,[13] in Shanghai, from which they watched political developments with increasing apprehension, especially as Borodin and Chiang Kai-shek (then a young military officer only beginning to win notice in Kuomintang circles) built up the Whampoa Cadet School and consolidated their military power.[14]

This split, together with increasing Communist influence within the Party, constituted a prime factor in shaping the nature of the Second National Congress and in bringing about a sharp upheaval in Central Executive Committee membership.

The Second Central Executive Committee

Elections for the Second CEC, in January 1926, brought defeat for those who had identified themselves with the Western Hills viewpoint (Chü Cheng, Tsou Lu, Hsiung K'e-wu, Lin Shen, Shih Ching-yang, T'an Cheng, Yang Hsi-min, and Yeh Ch'u-ts'ang), and victory for those who favored continued co-operation with the Soviet Union and close working relations with the Communist Party of China. Among the thirteen Committeemen re-elected from the 1924 Committee were a number of prominent Communist sympathizers, two Communists, and Hu Han-min, who had accepted many favors from the Russians in the first days of the alliance, but who, through the years, moved more and more toward the Western Hills group. To these incumbents were added at least four new Communist members and several pro-Communists, among whom the two widows, Mme. Sun Yat-sen and Mme. Liao Chung-k'ai, were especially notable (see Appendix B, Table 2).

Between the Second National Congress of January 1926 and the Third National Congress of March 1929, Kuomintang history was shaped to a remarkable degree by Chiang Kai-shek's increasing power and by his antagonism to the Communists. This conflict resulted in a party split, with a Kuomintang leftwing maintaining a short-lived Communist alliance in opposition to Chiang.[15]

The Third Central Executive Committee

Chiang Kai-shek effected two coups against the Communists, one in March 1926 and a second in April 1927. His preparations for the seizure of power followed two courses. Militarily, he established relations or working alliances with various individual officers, army cliques, and independent or semi-independent war lords. Politically, he encouraged the organization, under Ch'en Kuo-fu and Ch'en Li-fu, of an intra-Party faction which later, complete with police and intelligence arms, became the well-known Organization Group, or CC Clique. For a time the Kuomintang left-wing continued its alliance with the Reds, but by the beginning of 1928 thousands of Communists had been killed and the leaders had been driven underground.

The Third National Congress, which was opened on March 15, 1929, by Hu Han-min as Provisional Chairman and which remained in session thirteen days, elected a Central Executive Committee of thirty-six members whose political complexion was remarkably different from that of the 1926 membership. Certainly, there were no Communists on the 1929 Committee, and there were not many who could be accused of sympathizing with communism. At least one prominent Western Hills supporter, Yeh Ch'u-ts'ang, was reinstated with full membership (Appendix B, Table 3). Wang Ching-wei, opposing Chiang Kai-shek, allied himself first with T'ang Sheng-chih, a minor militarist, and later (1930) with Feng Yü-hsiang and Yen Hsi-shan.

At the time of this Congress, Chiang Kai-shek was probably the most powerful political and military leader in China, with tight control over Central Kuomintang Headquarters. For the next few years, however, he was to find himself unable to control his party and govern the country without allying himself with either Hu Han-min or Wang Ching-wei. It is significant, moreover, that the Standing Committee of the Central Executive Committee had decided as early as October 25, 1928, that the Central Party Headquarters should have power to name one-half of the delegates sent to the Third Congress by district Kuomintang organs.[16]

The six known Communists on the 1926 Committee had long since lost their seats on the Central Executive Committee, most of them disappearing — for the time being — without trace, and every effort was made by Chiang Kai-shek and his supporters (Ch'en Li-fu headed the intelligence section of the Kuomintang) to exclude other suspected Reds and their sympathizers from all positions of influence in the Party. Ch'en Kuo-fu, who with his brother, Ch'en Li-fu, was shaping the powerful anti-Communist CC Clique, was an important member of this Committee.

These factional conflicts, rather than preference changes on the part of any sort of Kuomintang electorate, determined the character of the Third Central Executive Committee. The period between the Third National Congress (March 1929) and the Fourth National Congress (November 1931) was marked by a long and complicated series of intra-Party intrigues, rebellions (such as those of Feng Yü-hsiang, Yen Hsi-shan, the Wang Ching-wei clique, and the Kwangsi militarists), and Communist uprisings, which somewhat weakened the power of Chiang Kai-shek.

A basic cause of these various conflicts was the fact that Chiang and the Nanking Government were able to maintain direct control over only those provinces near the mouth of the Yangtze River. In other areas, Nationalist authority rested upon a series of alliances with military men such as Feng Yü-hsiang in the Northwest, Yen Hsi-shan (who had extended his forces eastward from Shansi), and generals of the Kwangsi clique (such as Li Tsung-jen) who controlled the Hankow region.

Aggravating this fundamental instability were two other opposition groups with which Chiang Kai-shek was forced to cope: the Communists who, under Mao Tse-tung and Chu Te, were building soviets and a peasant Red Army in mountain districts of Hunan and Kiangsi; and the Reorganizationalists, or Kuomintang leftwingers grouped around Wang Ching-wei, who periodically accused Chiang of abandoning the revolutionary principles of Dr. Sun in favor of a personal military dictatorship.

The Fourth Central Executive Committee

To unify the Kuomintang in the face of Japanese aggression, it was decided during the autumn of 1931 that all members of the First, Second, and Third Central Executive Committees, with the exception of Communists, would automatically become members of the Fourth Central Executive Committee. To this group Chiang's Nanking party would add four new members, and the Canton branch, five new members (Appendix B, Table 5.).

At this point Chiang Kai-shek, who had alienated both Wang Ching-wei and Hu Han-min, did not enjoy the power, either within the Party or throughout China, which he had commanded at the time of the Third Congress. Of the seventy-two members of the CEC, about 15 percent seem to have been associated with the Ch'en brothers' CC Clique, or Organization Group, which came to control the Organization Department of the Party; about 9 percent (almost wholly military men) were considered personal affiliates of Chiang; and 4 percent were Whampoa graduates or allied military officers upon whom Chiang could count. In addition to these, there were a number of small factions consisting of former Western Hills leaders and other conservatives inclined toward Chiang. There was no certain unity, but possibly these groupings displayed more cohesion than was achieved by the feuding opposition of Hu Han-min and Wang Ching-wei.

It is fairly certain that the nature of this CEC, as in the case of the 1929 Committee, was determined to a large degree by conflicts of military force. Although both periods were marked by personal competition for power, the notable difference is that the 1926–29 struggles emphasized disagreements over the Communist question, whereas the 1929–31 antagonisms emphasized disagreements over problems which were largely of an intra-Kuomintang nature.

During the years between the Fourth and Fifth Congresses, an external factor— Japanese aggression— contributed to an increase in Chiang Kai-shek's power.

The compromise government of January 1932, hailed by many observers as a "progressive" one, included Sun Fo as Premier, Eugene Chen as Foreign Minister, and Ch'en Kung-po as Minister of Labor. Various liberal and left-wing circles expressed considerable approval of the fact that a change had been brought about by political, rather than military action. 17 But the subsequent records of some of its leaders, especially Ch'en Kung-po, who became a Japanese puppet, cast considerable doubt over their potentialities. In any case, the new combination was short-lived. With the departure of T. V. Soong from the Government, the flow of financial support from Shanghai banking circles diminished. Chiang Kai-shek, who had resigned from his office as President of the National Government, retired to his native village of Fenghua, and Wang Ching-wei and Hu Han-min refused to go to Nanking because of "ill health. " Under these circumstances, the Government under Sun Fo remained nearly helpless. Further, the Standing Committee never met, and the Canton leaders quickly formed three new organizations— the Southwest Executive Committee of the Kuomintang, the Southwest Political Council, and the Southwest Military Council— through which to channel their dissensions.

During this period Eugene Chen tried to initiate a policy of vigorous opposition to Japanese aggression, but both Chiang Kai-shek and Wang Ching-wei blocked these efforts, and since Ho Ying-ch'in, Chiang's appointee as Minister of War, remained in control over most of Nanking's military forces, the new administration (already short of funds) found itself unable to act against Japan.

Failing to achieve a change in Chinese policy toward Japan, Eugene Chen tendered his resignation. Thereupon Sun Fo went to Shanghai for the purpose of urging Chen to reconsider. But in the course of their conversations, Chen persuaded Sun to send in his own resignation. 18 This brought an end to the coalition movement. The fact was that the achievement of a unified government remained all but impossible without the participation of Chiang Kai-shek, who controlled the armed forces and had access to sources of finance.

Supported now by Wang Ching-wei, his former antagonist, and by the financial wizardry of T. V. Soong, Chiang regained power. To the Government were also added several members of an older generation of Chinese diplomats who had previously served under the northern militarists in Peking. V. K. Wellington Koo was perhaps representative of these men.

During the spring of 1932 a disagreement developed between Wang Ching-wei and Chang Hsüeh-liang, the young "Marshal of Manchuria," over the latter's conduct of operations against the Japanese. Wang, who later defected to the Japanese, maintained at this time that his opponent ought either to put up stubborn resistance against the invader or to resign in favor of a more able commander. Chang, on the other hand, argued that his troops were not sufficiently armed or adequately paid and that if Nanking wanted

more fighting, they should be willing to underwrite a campaign with arms
and money. In the midst of this situation, both men resigned their Nanking
posts and Wang set off for another of his health trips to Europe. For the
next three years, the various factions in the Kuomintang were in continual
conflict— often debates, sometimes abortive rebellions. Among the armed
struggles was the Fukien revolt. Three military leaders organized a
People's Government with a program for tariff autonomy, abolition of un-
equal treaties, freedom of strikes, religious liberty, state ownership of
lands, forests, and mines, and militant resistance against the Japanese.
Among the members of the new government were Eugene Chen, Li Chi-shen,
and Ts'ai T'ing-kai. Fukien leaders had hoped for support from Kwangtung
and Kwangsi militarists but this aid was not forthcoming, and after a brief
engagement with Nationalist forces the rebellion died. In the meantime,
Japanese troops captured Shankaikwan and, in February 1933, opened an
attack on Jehol.

The Fifth National Congress of the Kuomintang suffered two more post-
ponements before it was finally set for November 12, 1935. During the
twelve months preceding its convocation, the Japanese restored the Imperial
dynasty in Manchuria with P'u Yi upon the throne; Chiang Kai-shek inaugurated the New Life Movement, devoted to the rejuvenation of Confucian
teachings, and the Standing Committee of the Central Executive Committee
set August twenty-seventh as a national holiday in honor of Confucius. These
three separate events are in a sense symbolic of later developments important to the growing power of Chiang, namely, the advancing threat of
Japanese domination, the organization of extra-Party movements under the
leadership of Chiang and his affiliates, and the emphasizing of Confucianism
as a dynamic in economic, political, and social phases of Party and Government.

The Fifth Central Executive Committee

The Fifth National Congress of the Kuomintang, meeting between November 12 and November 23, 1935, comprised a total of 405 delegates from
various parts of China, including southern areas which at one time or another had supported the Canton separatist movement. Thus there was at
least an appearance of unity, with Chiang Kai-shek, Wang Ching-wei, Sun
Fo, Hu Han-min, and various of their supporters, all appearing on the new
Central Executive Committee of 120 members. However, the new body
could not claim even the impression of "progressiveness" which the 1931
Committee had offered.

The proportion of membership claimed by the Ch'en brothers' CC Clique,
by Chiang's personal affiliates, and by the Whampoa and related military
factions, had probably increased over 1931, while the percentage of Wang,
Sun Fo, and Eugene Chen supporters and allies seems to have diminished.
It is perhaps especially notable that Mme. Sun Yat-sen was shifted from
regular to reserve membership in the 1935 Committee.

Japanese expansion and the resultant years of war dominated developments within the Kuomintang during the period between the Fifth Congress in 1935 and the Sixth in 1945. This pressure of foreign aggression brought about two critical developments within the Chinese nation. The first of these was a new Kuomintang-Communist alliance; the second consisted of intra-Party unification within the Kuomintang itself.

In general, the Chinese Communists, rather than Chiang, were responsible for united-front action against Japan. For years — ever since April 1927 — both Russian and Chinese Communists had been denouncing Chiang as a reactionary, a tool of Western imperialists, a traitor deserving execution. Yet in the face of Japanese aggression, the Communist Party of China was forced to the conclusion that only Chiang could serve as a symbol for Chinese unity. By 1937, therefore, the Chinese Communist Party, developing a program begun in 1932, was demanding cessation of civil wars, the establishment of an anti-Japanese united front, and militant preparation for resistance against the invader.[19]

During the early years after the Japanese occupation of Mukden, Chiang, reluctant to take action against the aggressors while the Communists opposed him, had evoked bitter criticism from men like Hu Han-min (who, almost until the hour of his death in 1936, had called insistently for organized opposition to Tokyo). Finally, in December 1936, Chang Hsüeh-liang and other officers in command of troops charged with fighting Communists kidnaped Chiang at Sian and demanded military resistance against Japan.

Among Kuomintang leaders there had been no unity of opinion in regard to a Japanese policy, and the subsequent defection of Wang Ching-wei, Chou Fo-hai, and Ch'en Kung-po to the enemy camp makes a purely ideological analysis of various Chinese viewpoints nearly impossible.[20] But the Sian kidnaping incident, together with various related developments, convinced Chiang that leadership in China depended upon militant opposition to the invaders. The resulting Communist-Kuomintang alliance was an uneasy one at best, but it did allow Chiang respite in which to unify both Party and Government and to strengthen his power in China.

The CC Clique and Army factions loyal to Chiang steadily tightened their discipline over Kuomintang leadership. Of minor influence in the Party, but important in provincial echelons of the government, were members of the Political Science group who tended to represent business and financial interests and who were, on the whole, more moderate in their political attitudes and more clearly oriented toward the West than were members of the other two cliques.

During the Fifth National Congress a resolution had been passed to the effect that all civil servants should be required to study Party doctrine. Emphasis was placed upon the twelve rules of conduct set forth by the New Life Movement, which included loyalty, faithfulness, sincerity, obedience, and similar steadying virtues. Then, in July 1936, the Second Plenary Session of the Central Executive Committee had successfully abolished the Southwest Executive and the Southwest Political Council through which Hu Han-min and his followers had formerly expressed their opposition.

Next, in 1938, an Extraordinary Kuomintang National Congress elected Chiang Kai-shek Tsung-tsai, or Director-general, and endowed him with all the powers which Dr. Sun had enjoyed, including chairmanship of the Party Congress and of the Central Executive Committee, absolute right of veto over decisions of the Central Executive Committee, and suspensive veto over decisions of the Congress.

Further, in January 1939, the Fifth Plenary Session of the Central Executive Committee reorganized the Supreme National Defense Conference (which for more than a year had, in effect, directed all Party, political, and military affairs) into a Supreme National Defense Council under the chairmanship of the Tsung-tsai. In this new capacity, Chiang enjoyed emergency powers which exempted him from traditional Party procedures in handling both political and military affairs, and enabled him to issue such decrees as changing conditions might warrant. [21] Moreover, the principle of permitting the National Government to appoint representatives to the National Party Congress had been formalized in 1937 by the act of the Legislative Yuan. Chiang now enjoyed virtual control over both Party and Government. In accordance with this law, 240 of the 1,440 representatives (16.7 percent) constituting National Congress membership were to be designated by the National Government itself. [22]

The formation of auxiliary Kuomintang organizations served further to strengthen Chiang's position within the Party. Of these, the San Min Chu I Youth Corps is perhaps the best example. Founded for the expressed purposes of uniting and training young people, enforcing the San Min Chu I, defending the nation, and bringing about a national "rebirth," this organization was open to Chinese between sixteen and twenty-five years of age. Based on the principles of the New Life Movement, the Corps strove for rigid discipline. The Corps leader, according to its constitution, was the "Party Chief of the Kuomintang" (Chiang Kai-shek) with unrestricted powers of sanction and veto. [23] Chapter XIII of its 1938 Constitution laid down the following rules:[24]

66. All members should obey the following commandments:
    a. All questions may be freely discussed. But no dispute is allowed once the resolution is passed.
    b. It is not allowed to rebel against the principles of the New Life Movement.
    c. It is prohibited to reveal the secrets of the Corps.
    d. It is prohibited for members to join other organizations.
    e. It is prohibited to criticize unfavorably the Kuomintang and the Corps, or to plot against other members.
    f. It is prohibited to express one's ideas too freely upon current events, especially those that are against the resolved plans or policies of the Kuomintang or the Corps.
    g. It is prohibited to form other organizations within the Corps.
67. Those who are proved to act against the above rules will be punished in the following ways:

    <u>a</u>. warning
    <u>b</u>. demerit
    <u>c</u>. cross-questioning
    <u>d</u>. expulsion
    <u>e</u>. other appropriate punishments

Finally, as wartime measures, efforts were made to tighten Kuomintang Party controls. The first of these was the reintroduction of the Small Group, or Party cell (Hsiao-tsu). The second consisted of the further development of Party purging facilities through the Party Supervisor's Net (Tang-jen Chien-ch'a Wang).

All these measures — the organization of the New Life Movement, the abolition of the Southwest Political Conference, the granting of extraordinary powers to Chiang, the principle of designating a portion of the National Congress membership, the formation of auxiliary Party organizations, the reintroduction of Party Cells, and the working out of new devices for purging Party membership — are illustrative of the effect which the Japanese threat had upon the Kuomintang. They suggest, too, an inability on the part of Party organs to meet the wartime needs of China, and they are clearly indicative of the grip which Chiang and his supporters were able to obtain on Party machinery.

The Sixth Central Executive Committee

The Sixth National Congress of the Kuomintang, meeting between May 5 and May 21, 1945, comprised a total of 600 delegates plus the memberships of the Central Executive and Central Supervisory Committee. This body reelected Chiang Kai-shek as <u>Tsung</u>-<u>tsai</u>, and selected 222 members for the Central Executive Committee.

It had long been evident that Chiang Kai-shek and his organization had achieved a virtual monopoly of power within the Kuomintang. Of the new Central Executive Committee, 64.2 percent allegedly belonged to the CC Clique which, with its own police and intelligence arms, had sought control over vast sections of Party and Government machinery. In addition to CC members, it is estimated that about 6.3 percent of the Central Executive Committee membership were Chiang's personal affiliates, while a scattering of former Western Hills leaders, Whampoa graduates, and other military and political cliques lent further reliable support. These figures are by no means incontrovertible, since factional affiliation, based often on reports that are scarcely more than rumor, is difficult to fix. In this case it is significant, however, that a CC-sponsored resolution which required all delegates to sign their ballots in CEC elections was passed and put into effect during the Sixth Congress.

There was, then (and this will be indicated more graphically in Section IV), a power balance, presided over by Chiang Kai-shek, between civilian Party organizers on the one hand and military men on the other. Neither had a monopoly of power, but Chiang Kai-shek, being in a position to use one group as a check on the activities of the other, enjoyed the loyalty — and the accumulated power — of both.

Over-all Trends

In view of the long record of unrest in China during the period under consideration, in view of the professed revolutionary nature of the Kuomintang, and in view of the importance which military strength played in the struggle for power, Party leadership seems to have been remarkably secure in office. Central Committeemen (with the exception of unwavering Communists) were re-elected by one Congress after another, or, if dropped (as in the case of the Western Hills leaders in 1926), they almost invariably reappeared as the result of some later realignment or political truce. There was, moreover, a minimum of intra-Party bloodshed (except for the numerous executions of Communists) resulting from the various struggles for power.

At the time of the Sixth National Congress nearly 90 percent of the previous Committee members were still alive, and almost all, with the exception of the Communists, held positions of leadership in the Party. Of the seventeen deaths recorded, two resulted from assassination (neither case was satisfactorily accounted for), and two men were executed (one for deserting to Japan, one for "graft in office"). The rest died more or less peacefully of old age or from various diseases of the flesh.

In a narrow sense, the total of these trends, together with events of historical record, suggests that the development of the Central Executive Committee elite after 1926 cannot be separated from Chiang's personal rise to power. In this connection, there is good reason for believing that in 1929 his power was derived largely from victories of the Northern Expedition, but that in succeeding years the balance was more precarious, depending upon the juxtaposition of various independent or semi-independent political factions and military cliques in relation to power.

But the Japanese accumulation of power in northern China tended to redress this balance to Chiang's advantage. For the Japanese threat, more than any other single element, brought about a working, if uneasy, alliance between Kuomintang and Communist parties; secured emergency powers for Chiang; obtained foreign loans; and provided exactly the secret, wartime-emergency environment in which police and intelligence functions could most easily and properly be expanded. In short, it was to a considerable degree the Japanese threat which made Chiang Kai-shek the recognized leader of wartime China, from Yenan and Chungking to Washington and Moscow.

If this analysis is correct, then the size and composition of the Central Executive Committee (never a representative body in the Western, parliamentary sense) were, especially after 1931, symptomatic, rather than critical political factors; had little to do with the true wishes of rank-and-file Kuomintang members; and bore almost no relationship whatsoever to the will of the general population of China. Increases in Chiang's power within the Kuomintang can be explained largely in terms of two factors: the Japanese threat, and the weakness of the Kuomintang in the face of the overwhelming needs of China.

III. THE DEVELOPMENT OF THE CHINESE
COMMUNIST PARTY LEADERSHIP

The current Chinese Communist leadership represents the culmination
of thirty years of growth, a complex development which can be divided into
four main phases: the leadership of Ch'en Tu-hsiu (1918−August 1927);
the period of urban insurrection (August 1927−January 1931); the returned
student leadership (January 1931−January 1935); and the rise of Mao Tse-
tung from January 1935 until the present.

It is not easy to assemble precise information about the various leadership groups, nor to determine exactly what changes took place. To date,
the only full Central Committee membership rolls are those of recent
years, and most Politburo lists are admittedly incomplete. [25] Because of
this faulty documentation one can only assemble and piece together whatever data are available with the hope that future research may fill in present gaps and correct current misconceptions.

If it is difficult to document developments in leadership, it is nearly impossible to document adequately the revolution which these leaders succeeded in capturing. Many observers, Western as well as Chinese, have described phases of the agrarian unrest and agrarian uprisings which Mao and
his followers gradually harnessed. Communist documents indicate that Red
leaders— especially during the period 1928−1934— were disturbed by the
fact that other groups and other leaders (including Wang Ching-wei and
even Chiang Kai-shek) were themselves trying to win over the peasantry
with its spontaneous revolutionary dynamic. But these are indirect and
loosely worded descriptions of an upheaval that could have been measured
adequately only by specialized techniques in the hands of specialized in-
vestigators there at the time. Unfortunately, there were no teams of econo-
mists, sociologists, or anthropologists roaming the hills of Hunan and
Kiangsi during the years when agrarian unrest broke into agrarian revolt.
Because of this, we are now inclined all too often to confuse the sometimes
mute, sometimes amorphous, but potentially dynamic masses of dissatisfied peasantry with the tightly organized, conspiratorial, often Moscow-
trained leadership which gradually won control of them.

No attempt is made here to isolate causes of mass discontent or to ana-
lyze dynamic forces released by peasants in revolt against traditional social
structures. Rather, this study seeks to investigate only the higher echelons
of Communist leadership— the changes it has undergone, its interrelation-
ships, and some of its contacts with central Party headquarters in Moscow.

The Leadership of Ch'en Tu-hsiu: 1918−August 1927

It was the impact of the Russian Revolution on China which opened the
first phase by impressing upon certain Chinese radical leaders the promise
of Marxism as a key to solving China's national problems and later the
value of Leninist tactics for the exploitation of indigenous discontent. Within a year after the Russian Revolution of October 1917, Marxist circles

had been organized among certain intellectual groups in China. At Peking University the dean of the College of Literature, Ch'en Tu-hsiu, and the chief librarian, Li Ta-chao, founded such groups. A student named Mao Tse-tung organized a similar one at Changsha. Ch'en Tu-hsiu, in order to unify these tendencies, next gathered together a group of potential revolutionists and began publication of <u>Mei-chou P'ing-lun</u>, a periodical weekly newspaper dedicated to radical thinking. By the beginning of 1919, Soviet Russian leaders had begun expressing interest in the possibility of helping to organize an effective revolutionary government in southern China.

In the spring of 1920 the Comintern dispatched two agents, Voitinsky and an overseas Chinese named Yang Ming-chai, to help organize the Chinese Communist movement. On reaching Peking, Voitinsky made contact with Li Ta-chao, who then introduced him to a Shanghai literary group to which Ch'en Tu-hsiu belonged. In that city he set up his headquarters and began organizational work. Unable to gather together a group of true Communists, he assembled a number of leftists of varying shades and founded the Chinese Socialist Youth Club. This, and subsequent organizational work, was done with such secrecy that even the British Intelligence Service is said to have been unaware of the presence of Russian agents in China until nearly two years later.

This group consisted of about eight original members. As soon as it was set up, similar cells were established elsewhere. Chang Kuo-t'ao organized one in Peking, Mao Tse-tung started one in Hunan, and Tung Pi-wu formed one in Hupeh. At about the same time four Chinese students established a cell in Japan, while others, including Chou En-lai and Li Li-san, formed one in Paris.

In Shanghai Ch'en Tu-hsiu and his comrades started the Communist Youth Association with about a hundred members, began publishing two Bolshevik organs, and organized a so-called "School of Foreign Languages" in order to prepare the best revolutionaries for work in China and for study at the Communist University of the Far East in Soviet Russia. In 1920 the enrollment at this foreign language school consisted of about sixty students, most of whom belonged to the Communist Youth League.

Early in 1921 a war lord named Ch'en Chiung-ming seized control of Kwangtung Province and invited Dr. Sun Yat-sen to return to Canton. Somewhat previously Ch'en Tu-hsiu had attracted the attention of Ch'en Chiung-ming,[26] who now asked the Communist organizer to serve as chief of the Education Board in Canton. Ch'en Tu-hsiu accepted with alacrity, explaining to Voitinsky that he would take the job and use it for purposes of Communist propaganda. Once installed in his new position, Ch'en Tu-hsiu oversaw the formation of a Communist cell in Canton and the setting up of a school for party organizers and propagandists. Later in the year he returned to Shanghai where he joined forces with a prominent Kuomintang revolutionist named Tai Chi-t'ao. Shortly after his arrival there, however, he was imprisoned by German authorities. Subsequently, after his

release had been effected, Ch'en Tu-hsiu co-operated with Tai Chi-t'ao
in revolutionary activities. Working together, they organized trade unions,
published a number of different newspapers and periodicals of left-wing
complexion, and gradually succeeded in assembling about them the nucleus
of what was later to develop into the Communist Party of China.

During this first year of activity, a number of splits occurred in the
new Communist movement. For the most part, this difficulty arose from
the fact that many of the early members considered themselves anarchists,
rather than Bolsheviks. The first break took place within the Peking cell
while a provisional party statute was under discussion. One paragraph
dealt with the dictatorship of the proletariat, a concept which the anarchists
refused to accept, and many of them, therefore, left the movement. [27]

The Chinese Communists held their First Congress in Shanghai during
the last week of July 1921.(Appendix C, Table 2). Thirteen representatives
spoke for about fifty members of the Communist Party nuclei of Peking,
Tientsin, Hunan, Hupeh, Shantung, and Kwangtung. Each area had elected
two representatives, and one had been sent from the cell in Japan. The
Comintern had at least one agent present, a Hollander named Maring.

The first acknowledged head of the Chinese Communist Party, Ch'en
Tu-hsiu, was forty-one years old at the time of the First Congress. Born
in Anhwei of a wealthy Mandarin family, he had studied naval architecture
in Chekiang and had later continued his education in France. In 1915 he
launched Hsin ch'ing-nien (La Jeunesse), a review demanding the introduction into China of Western ideas, the opposing of traditional Chinese ideas,
and the elimination of Confucianism. Two years later he was appointed
dean of the College of Literature at the University of Peking, and it was
while serving in this position that he was first attracted by Leninist ideas.
Ch'en was dismissed from the Chinese Communist Party after the Kuomintang-Communist alliance failed in 1927. Sentenced in 1932 to fifteen years
imprisonment by the Kuomintang, he was released during the Japanese
war and died thereafter.

At least five of the thirteen delegates to the First Congress were alive
in 1949, but only two— Mao Tse-tung and Tung Pi-wu— were still prominent
in the Communist Party. Of the rest, Ho Shu-heng was shot by the Kuomintang in 1927; Chou Fo-hai left the Communist Party and, in February 1948,
died of a heart attack in a Chinese prison; Ch'en Kung-po also left the
Communist Party and, in June 1946, was executed for treason. Chang Kuo-
t'ao, long a powerful figure in the Communist Party, was expelled in 1938
and was elected in 1945 to the Sixth Executive Committee of the Kuomintang.
The remaining three disappeared from sight at one time or another, and
no information concerning their fates is available.

This Congress reflected the real composition of the Chinese Communist
movement at the time. For despite recent upheavals in various cells, the
delegates still included followers of what were called "biblical socialism,
social democracy, anarchism and various shades of communism."[28]

Unable to attend the meeting, Ch'en Tu-hsiu sent a carefully drawn-up and relatively moderate program for consideration by the delegates. His proposals included plans for educating party members, for encouraging a "democratic" spirit, for developing party discipline, and for making cautious contacts with the masses. The time was not ripe, he maintained, for the party to consider a seizure of power, and consequently, the movement should confine itself to preparatory activities. [29]

The various delegations found themselves in immediate disagreement over Ch'en's proposals. Some thought them too radical, while others wanted more precipitate action. One delegate pointed out that in Germany and Russia there had been separate revolutionary movements — one pointing toward democracy, the other toward a dictatorship of the proletariat. Why not send representatives to study both situations and report back with their findings?

According to subsequent accounts, however, "a decisive resistance was shown to all these dangerous currents" and most of Ch'en's proposals were accepted in a "positive sense."[30] It was determined that the movement should henceforth consider itself a Communist Party, that its work should follow Communist principles, and that the final aim of this work should be the organization of the proletariat and the seizure of power by the laboring masses under Party guidance. The Congress further decreed that thereafter all members of the movement who were holding non-Communist views were to be purged from the Party.

Before the close of this Congress, the delegates resolved to co-operate with Dr. Sun Yat-sen through extra-party support. There was some "ultra-leftist" opposition from those who maintained that Communists could not logically support middle-class revolutionary movements under any circumstance and who insisted that a dictatorship of the proletariat should be set up immediately. But support for Dr. Sun was entirely in line with tactics which Lenin had laid down at the Second Congress of the Communist International less than a year earlier, and the resolution was passed.[31]

Early Communist Party Structure

The First Congress of the Chinese Communist Party erected the skeletal framework of what grew into a full-sized Communist Party structure. During the early years after the Bolshevik Revolution in Russia the Comintern and the Communist Party of the Soviet Union developed a system of Party organization pyramiding upward from the factory (and street) nucleus and the Party fraction. According to rules laid down by the Third International, all Communists working in a single factory or other place of labor must belong to the nucleus of that particular place. Members of this group were then required to elect an executive committee of between three and five members.

In cities where numerous factories existed, all nuclei were united into subsections which, in turn, were welded into sections. All the sections in a given city constituted a local Party organization, and thus the various organs pyramided upward through national and international levels. In each

stratum membership was charged with electing the next higher organ, except when the Communist Party was illegal, in which case the whole system
might be streamlined for security purposes. In line with principles of
"democratic centralism," no opposition to a majority opinion was tolerated
once a decision had been reached.

The tasks of the factory nucleus were laid down precisely by the Comintern. Members were specifically held responsible for the conduct of Communist agitation and propaganda among workers; for the instruction of non-
Communist laborers in order to draw them into Bolshevik ranks; for the
discussion of factory problems with all the workers; for the issuance of a
special factory newspaper; for participation in and leadership of demonstra-
tions and strikes; for pointing out to fellow workers the political consequences of the labor struggle; and for carrying on an obstinate fight in all
factories against other parties, especially non-Bolshevik socialists and
other antagonistic labor groups.

The Party fraction served a different purpose. Whereas the nucleus
formed an organizational basis for the whole Party structure, the fraction
had a much more specialized function, namely, to infiltrate and, where
necessary, to capture other already existing organizations such as labor
unions, factory committees, strike committees, congresses, parliaments,
and similar organizations. [32] According to Comintern regulations, it was
mandatory, in any organization where there were three or more Communists,
to form a fraction for the increase of "Party influence" and for the introduction of "Party policy into non-Party masses."[33]

The strength of the fraction depended upon two regulations. First, every
question subject to the decision of a non-Party body or institution must be
discussed and decided upon at an earlier meeting of the parasite fraction.
And second, all fraction members must act and vote as a unit on all questions within meetings of the non-Party body or institution.

During 1921 the Chinese Communist Party structure did not progress
beyond the formative stages, and existing accounts are so contradictory
that it is nearly impossible to determine the exact nature of its leadership.
There is, for example, considerable disagreement concerning the size
and membership of the First Central Committee. It has been said that all
delegates to the First Congress were included upon the First Committee.
But Mao Tse-tung, in an interview with Edgar Snow a decade and a half
later, presented a different membership list (Appendix C, Table 2).

The Communist-Kuomintang Alliance

During the early months after the First Congress, the Chinese Communist
Party carried on its activities independently and, in accordance with deci-
sions reached at the Congress, offered only extra-Party support to Dr. Sun
Yat-sen and the Kuomintang. But it soon became clear to certain Communist
leaders both in Moscow and in China that neither the Chinese Communist
Party nor the Kuomintang was acting with maximum effectiveness. Dr. Sun

had a larger following than the Communists, but his party lacked the organization and discipline which Leninist advisers could presumably supply.[34]
Therefore, at a Special Plenum of the Central Committee of the Chinese
Communist Party in August 1922, Maring invoked the authority of the Comintern to persuade the Chinese Communists that their membership must
infiltrate or invade the Kuomintang.

Ch'en Tu-hsiu may have opposed this Communist-Kuomintang alliance.
"Myself and other Central Committee members . . . were opposed," he
wrote later, "because the conglomeration of forces within the Kuomintang
blurred class distinctions, thus checking our independent policy. Maring
(representing the Comintern) countered by asking if we wanted to disobey
a Comintern decision, so that the Central Committee gave in for the sake
of party discipline and voted to join the Kuomintang."[35]

Maring had his way. But after Ch'en Chiung-ming had effected his rebellion against Dr. Sun, Red leaders decided that more active measures
must be taken. The Communist Party consequently sent representatives
to confer with Sun and to propose united front action against enemies of
the Kuomintang. Sun, discouraged by defeat and by weaknesses within the
Kuomintang, accepted and, at that particular time, even some of his rightist followers approved.

A long series of negotiations was necessary, however, before the Communist Party and the Kuomintang were able to come to a working agreement.
From the Red viewpoint, Dr. Sun's Kuomintang suffered two basic weaknesses. First, it was clear to Communist observers in Russia and China
alike that the Kuomintang was dependent upon foreign help for the completion of its revolution. And second, the Kuomintang, considering military
action the only means of furthering the revolution, had concentrated all its
efforts on military affairs, thus neglecting to reach the masses through
propaganda.

Bolshevik leaders in Moscow decided, therefore, to negotiate directly
with Sun in order to make the Kuomintang a more effective force. In January 1923 Adolph Joffe, who had been treating unsuccessfully with the Peking
Government, was directed to stop off in the course of a trip to Japan for
conversations with Dr. Sun in Shanghai. The result of these discussions
was the signing of a joint statement in which the Bolshevik representative
agreed with the Kuomintang leader that neither the Communist order nor
the soviet system could be introduced into China under existing conditions,
but that the primary problem was one of national unification and independence.

Joffe reaffirmed earlier Soviet renunciations of all Czarist treaties,
privileges, and exactions and expressed willingness to negotiate on a basis
of equality. This understanding was followed by further negotiations, and
in June 1923 the Manifesto of the Third Congress of the Chinese Communist
Party recognized the Kuomintang as "the central force of the revolution"
and urged "all revolutionary elements" to rally to the Kuomintang. The
Communist mission was defined, however, in terms of "liberating" the

Chinese people and advancing the world revolution.[36] Related to these policies was an understanding between Sun and the Soviet Union whereby Moscow sent arms, ammunition, and money to the Canton Government, and subsequently an advisory mission under a veteran Bolshevik agent, Michael Borodin.

When Borodin arrived in Canton in September 1923 he found the Kuomintang disorganized, the workers divided, and the peasants a-political. Sun himself was so short of military supplies as to be utterly helpless against neighboring war lords and without hope for immediate prosecution of a revolution. But now, with the aid of Russian funds and a cadre of Russian experts, Borodin reorganized the Kuomintang, established the Whampoa Military Academy to train officers for Sun's armies, negotiated an alliance between the Soviet Union and the Canton Government, and made arrangements for the shipment of military supplies from the U.S.S.R. to China by way of Vladivostok.

At the same time the Chinese Communist Party worked not only within the Kuomintang, but also within student, labor, and similar movements with which it was now in legal contact. On paper, at least, the Chinese Communists and the Third International wove all these activities into a revolutionary network which extended over China from north to south. It included not only Borodin, but also the Soviet ambassador to the Peking Government, Karakhan, and the newly established Soviet diplomatic agencies, and was responsible to Comintern discipline and to Russian secret police surveillance.

To Communists—Chinese and Russian alike—the overthrow of the Peking Government, the expulsion of foreign imperialists, and the victory of national revolutionary forces in China were inevitable developments within the dialectic struggle which Marx had prophesied and for which Lenin had systematized a whole manual of detailed strategies and tactics. Yet within the following three years quite the opposite came about: Borodin and his assistants were eliminated from the Kuomintang; the Third International's Chinese program failed; Chiang won control of the Kuomintang and killed or drove underground thousands of Chinese Communists; and topmost leaders of the world Communist movement found themselves groping for the reason. In many respects this unexpected failure was facilitated by the deaths of two men—Sun and Lenin.

The analysis of Kuomintang leadership has suggested the intra-Party ferment and intrigue brought about by Sun's passing. The death of Lenin loosed a series of much more deadly conflicts. To a large degree, these conflicts resulted from the personal struggle for power between Stalin and Trotsky, a feud that opened a schism cutting all the way from Moscow to the nuclei and fractions in China.[37] With regard to Asia, however, serious conflicts also emerged from the essential contradiction between Roy's emphasis on the development of class conflict, and Lenin's concept of a Communist alliance with middle-class revolutionary movements like the Kuomintang. The Second Congress had tied these antagonistic concepts into a single policy which Borodin, his colleagues and subordinates, and the Chinese Communist Party were now charged with carrying out.

In February 1926 Borodin left Canton for northern China, ostensibly to negotiate with the so-called "Christian general," Feng Yü-hsiang, but also, according to some observers, for the purpose of meeting with a Comintern investigating commission. Whether or not the latter was his purpose, there is no question about the rift which had appeared in China between those like Borodin and Ch'en Tu-hsiu, who wanted to work slowly through the Kuomintang, and others who wanted to accelerate the development of a peasant and working-class revolution.

Conflict raged especially among those Communists who were working through Kuomintang army fractions and the peasant movement. [38] Jay Calvin Huston, an American consular official, reported subsequently that the chief of the Russian military group at Canton had complained to Karakhan that activities of Communist agitators in Nationalist armies were antagonizing Kuomintang officers. [39] The consular official supported this view with a report from another Soviet agent who charged that Communist organizers (Russian and Chinese) were centralizing their control over the armies with dangerous haste. The Reds were trying to spread Bolshevik ideas too fast, he said, by rooting out the Kuomintang "always and everywhere" and thus creating opposition which strengthened the position of Chiang and other Nationalist leaders. [40]

Many revolutionists denounced this viewpoint, asserting that Borodin and Ch'en Tu-hsiu had compromised with the bourgeoisie, had submitted to Chiang Kai-shek, and had betrayed the revolution. To paraphrase Harold R. Isaacs' much later criticism of Borodin's tactics: Chiang wrapped himself in radical phrases and presented himself to Borodin and to the masses as the Red hope of the revolutionary army. Borodin therefore employed every possible political stratagem to drive Chiang to the top of the heap. Chiang, in turn, quoted Sun that in taking Borodin's advice, he was taking Sun's advice. And Borodin said that no matter whether Communist or Kuomintang, all must obey Chiang. [41]

Huston, who was staunchly anti-Communist, but who respected Borodin as an individual, wrote on the other hand that the Comintern agent knew exactly what he was doing. "Borodin had dreamed of five years in which he hoped to have the laborers and peasants of Kwangtung organized into a revolutionary force that would sweep over China. But the impetuosity of Communist leaders in the Kuomintang and their Russian confreres upset his plans and made it necessary to compromise with a leader who had a growing ambition to dominate the Chinese situation in a military way."

According to Huston, these "impetuous" Communist leaders were convinced that the time had come for seizing Canton as one objective in an imminent world revolution, whereas Borodin (supported by Ch'en Tu-hsiu) actually understood the realities of the situation, "his object being to create a strong revolutionary base under Kuomintang rule." [42]

In retrospect it appears that, in terms of their own self-interests, both groups erred. The former, by pushing for an immediate Bolshevik revolution, probably strengthened Chiang and facilitated his coups against the Chinese Communists and the Kuomintang. The latter — especially Borodin and Ch'en Tu-hsiu — seem on the other hand, to have trusted in Chiang with unbelievable naïveté.

While Borodin was in the north treating with Feng Yü-hsiang (and facing, perhaps, a Comintern investigating commission), Chiang Kai-shek accomplished his coup of March 20, 1926. This should have been warning enough to the Communists that the Kuomintang general was not a docile ally. Yet Stalinist reactions seem to have been confined largely to the issuance of denials that such a coup had ever taken place.

Although Chiang proceeded to disqualify Communists from serving as the heads of departments under the Central Executive Committee of the Kuomintang and from filling other posts of responsibility within his party, Borodin, on his return from the north, accepted all restrictions upon himself and his fellow Communists and compromised his position even further by "appointing" Chiang Commander in Chief of the Northern Expedition with extraordinary powers over military, political, and Kuomintang party organs and functions. [43] According to the Comintern, this policy of further co-operation was undertaken in order to "prevent unification between Chiang Kai-shek and the Right wing" by making concessions to him. [44]

A year later Chiang's troops, aided by Russian supplies and by the coordinated agitation and organizational activities of the Chinese Communists, neared Shanghai; whereupon the Communist-controlled General Labor Union in the city called a strike, disarmed the garrison, and welcomed Kuomintang troops, who were thus able to enter without resistance from enemy forces.

At the time when Shanghai Communists were handing the city over to Chiang, the foreign quarter buzzed with rumors to the effect that the Kuomintang leader was preparing for a second coup. Reports indicated that he had organized an intra-Party police force of his own and that he was negotiating with Shanghai banking circles for a loan.

Following their tactics of the preceding year, Russian Communists denied these stories. A split within the Kuomintang was absolutely out of the question, they said. A revolutionary like Chiang Kai-shek could not possibly co-operate with counterrevolutionists, [45] and in any case, the "revolutionary pressure from below" was so strong that Chiang was being compelled to swear allegiance to the principles of revolutionary loyalty and to "submit himself" to the leadership of the "mass party of the Kuomintang." [46]

Chiang, less than a month later, launched his "Purification Movement" which, within the first few days of its prosecution, wiped out the Communist-controlled labor movement in Shanghai and, according to Communist estimates, cost the lives of 600 Chinese "proletarians." [47] And concurrently Chiang negotiated a substantial loan from financiers in Shanghai, inaugurated in Nanking a new Kuomintang Central Executive Committee and a new National Government, and prepared for a further extension of his power.

During the late spring of 1927 Stalinist theoreticians in Moscow were describing Chiang's coup as a foreseen and dialectically inevitable event marking the end of one phase of the Chinese conflict and the beginning of a new one which called for the confiscation and nationalization of land. This did not mean that the Chinese Communists should leave the Wuhan (or Hankow) Kuomintang under Wang Ching-wei and his colleagues. On the contrary, Chinese Reds were instructed "to take a leading role" within the Kuomintang left wing. They were to encourage the Wuhan government to release the agrarian revolt and change itself into an "organizational-political center of the workers and peasants revolution" and into an organ of the "democratic dictatorship of the proletariat and peasantry."[48]

A section of Chinese Communist leadership headed by Ch'en Tu-hsiu and T'an P'ing-shan opposed the vigorous prosecution of so radical an agrarian program on the ground that, since many Kuomintang leaders, both left wing and right, and many officers in the Kuomintang army were landholders or the sons of landholders, a policy of widespread confiscation might drive a wedge between them and the Communist Party. Ch'en Tu-hsiu, while admitting that the Communist agrarian program had been "too peaceful," warned that the confiscation of large and middle-size landed estates must await further development of the military situation. "The only correct solution at the present moment," he told the Fifth Congress of the Chinese Communist Party in April 1927, "is to deepen the revolution after it has first been spread."[49] In line with this viewpoint, Chinese Communist officials actively restrained a spontaneous peasant outbreak at Changsha in May 1927 and co-operated with Kuomintang leftists in attempts to eliminate other "anarchic" conditions in the villages.[50]

But Communist leaders in Moscow, despite the fact that their policies had been based upon continued co-operation with the Kuomintang Left, insisted that the time for peasant agitation had arrived. "Without an agrarian revolution, victory is impossible," Stalin wired his agents in China in late May 1927.[51] Certain old leaders of the Central Committee of the Kuomintang, he stated, were afraid of what was taking place. Consequently, the Communists must arrange for drawing a large number of peasant and working-class leaders into the Wuhan Government to change the structure of the Kuomintang, for setting up a military tribunal to punish those maintaining contact with Chiang or attacking workers and peasants, and for raising a reliable army of about 20,000 Communists and 50,000 revolutionary workers and peasants before it was "too late."

On June 1, 1927, this telegram was brought to the attention of Wang Ching-wei who, with expressions of extreme consternation,[52] took immediate action against Borodin and the Chinese Communists. Within a few weeks the former was on his way back to the Soviet Union, and Chinese Communists were hiding out wherever they could escape detection.

The Period of Urban Insurrection: August 1927–January 1931

The second period in the development of Chinese Communist leadership began on August 7, 1927, with the calling of a Special Conference which, on advice from Moscow, censured the Chinese Central Committee for carrying out "an opportunistic policy of betrayal," deposed Ch'en Tu-hsiu, and reorganized the whole Party hierarchy. A resólution adopted by the Conference stated:

> We welcome the energetic intervention of the Comintern which en-
> abled us to expose the mistakes of the previous Party leadership
> and thus save the Party. We emphatically condemn the opportunist,
> non-revolutionary policy pursued by our Central Committee and
> consider it necessary, on the basis of lessons of the past, radical-
> ly to change the course of Party policy.[53]

An important reason for past mistakes, the Conference decided, was that leadership had been generally in the hands of intelligentsia and bour-geoisie. Only upon the insistence of the Comintern, according to the August 7 Manifesto of the Party, had a few workers been admitted to the central hierarchy, whereas the Central Committee had often discriminated against workers on the grounds that their cultural standards were too low.

The Special Conference condemned Ch'en Tu-hsiu and T'an P'ing-shan for stating that the revolution must be spread before it could be deepened, severely criticized the policy of restraining the peasants, and censured the leadership for "retreating temporarily in order to retain the alliance with the Kuomintang."

Concurrently, the Special Conference, in line with a policy initiated by Stalin, decided against a Communist withdrawal from the Left Kuomintang. Supporting a Moscow resolution to the effect that the Communist Party "must take all necessary measures to arouse the lower strata of the Left Kuomintang against the upper,"[54] the Chinese leadership promised to "fight this struggle [against militarists, imperialists, and feudalists] with the really revolutionary members of the Kuomintang and with the masses of the Kuomintang." In the words of a Chinese resolution, the Communists had "no reason to leave the Kuomintang or to refuse to cooperate with it."[55]

Within a few weeks the error in this tactic became evident, as we shall see below. For if there had ever been any possibility of arousing the "lower strata" of the Kuomintang Left against the upper, that time had passed. The whole plan failed, whereupon, less than a year later, the Comintern (without criticizing Stalin, its own Executive Committee, or the Russian Communist Party) was exposing a serious error on the part of the Special Conference of the Chinese Communist Party: it had raised false hopes for the emergence of a left revolutionary Kuomintang and had actually called for action under such a banner![56]

The fact was that after the failure of this tactic, no one wanted to take responsibility for it. Nearly a decade later Mao Tse-tung, who by then had risen to leadership of the Chinese Communist Party, told Edgar Snow that at the Special Conference "all hope of cooperation with the Kuomintang was given up for the present . . . "[57]

There is no official Central Committee membership list available for the period, but the ruling clique is said to have consisted of Li Li-san, Hsiang Chung-fa, Ch'ü Ch'iu-pai, Chou En-lai, Li Wei-han, and Liu Shao-ch'i. Officially, Ch'ü Ch'iu-pai succeeded Ch'en Tu-hsiu as Secretary General of the Party,[58] but some sources indicate that activities were largely undertaken by Li Li-san, while actual power throughout the autumn of 1927 stemmed from two Comintern agents, Heinz Neumann and Besso Lominadze.[59]

The mood of the new leadership was for action to replace the caution which Ch'en Tu-hsiu had displayed. Six days prior to the opening of the Special Conference a Communist uprising "under the banner of the Kuomintang Left" had taken place at Nanchang when Red elements under Yeh Ting, Ho Lung (commander in chief of the 20th Kuomintang Army) and Chu Te carried out a successful mutiny within the "ironsides," the best army corps in Kuomintang service, and thus brought into Communist ranks a reported total of nearly 20,000 men.[60]

This victory was hailed as the beginning of a new revolutionary upsurge, whereupon a "drive to the sea" was initiated, and from September 24 to October 2 the city of Swatow lay under Communist control. But before long the whole revolutionary army, because of "the superiority of reactionary militarists and its own wrong tactics" was in full retreat.[61] This was the beginning of the end for the "Kuomintang Left" line of the Comintern; yet two days before the retreat began, Pravda was still hailing temporary successes as a "new revolutionary upsurge." The Kuomintang Left had been successfully exploited, one editorial maintained, and had brought about the beginning of a new phase — the formation of soviets.[62] But as soon as it became clear that the rebellion had actually failed, responsibility was pinned — not on Stalin or his agents or the "ruling clique" — but on T'an P'ing-shan, who was denounced and expelled for his "Kuomintang Left illusions."[63]

Depending now on a strategy of urban insurrections, Lominadze and Neumann still hoped for quick revolutionary successes in China.

By November 1927 power in Canton was being shared by two rival generals, Li Chi-shen and Chang Fa-kuei. The latter, with support from Wang Ching-wei, was now planning a coup for complete control of the city. It was this situation which Neumann and his associates were planning to exploit. Tactics were laid out on paper and arrangements made for setting up a Soviet of Workers', Soldiers' and Peasants' Deputies.

Two days before the insurrection, Canton police uncovered the plot and issued a directive for the arrest of all Communist leaders, whereupon Red forces, acting quickly, seized policy headquarters, barracks, and post and telegraph offices, and set up a "Soviet regime." But fresh elements of Chang Fa-kuei's troops soon entered the city, while fleet units opened a bombardment, and before long the "Canton Commune" fell. Neumann and Lominadze were recalled to Moscow where Stalin called them personally to task.[64]

Stalin now described the situation in China as a trough between two
waves, but he, as well as the Chinese Communist Party leadership, claimed
to foresee an imminent revolutionary upsurge which the Bolsheviks could
exploit. During the latter months of 1928 the Sixth Congress of the Third
International, while reaffirming Lenin's theses for revolution in backward
countries, laid out for China a program of armed insurrection essentially
similar to the plan which had failed at Canton as the "sole path to the completion of bourgeois democratic revolution" and to the overthrow of the
Kuomintang. [65] After a long series of preparatory directives addressed to
the Central Committee of the Chinese Communist Party, the Comintern
in October 1929 dispatched a letter calling for action under this program.

There were three primary premises for Moscow's decision to push a
policy of armed insurrection at this time: an acceleration of peasant guerrilla warfare in widespread rural areas; an increase in the number and intensity
of rebellions against Chiang Kai-shek (such as those of Feng Yü-hsiang,
Yen Hsi-shan, the Wang Ching-wei clique, and the Kwangsi militarists);
and an allegedly imminent and violent upsurge among labor masses. [66]

Moscow, in the same directive, issued decisive orders to the Chinese
Communist Party for the carrying out of the insurrectionary program:
consolidate and expand guerrilla warfare; develop political strikes; turn
the "fratricidal war" (the Fukien Rebellion and others) into a class war;
and transform peasant struggles into urban insurrections.

When this policy failed during the latter half of 1930, it was to Li Li-san
that responsibility for defeat was assigned. And while it was undoubtedly
true that Li Li-san did act precipitously, pushing ahead faster than Moscow's
directives had intended and committing tactical errors within the framework of Comintern strategy, there is also strong evidence of three fundamental and critical misconceptions on the part of Moscow.

The first of these misconceptions pertained to the nature of peasant
guerrilla warfare and its relation to the revolution in China. For Stalinists,
despite their emphasis upon the necessity for building a peasant army, still
viewed agrarian revolution as a subsidiary part of the total Chinese upheaval. If at any given time the urban workers needed an army, the peasantry
could provide it. And if at any time the urban workers were too weakened
by defeat to act, the peasantry might even be allowed to take momentary
initiative. But according to Moscow, insurrections begun in villages must
be transported to the cities, to the big industrial centers, for the establishment of an urban-based Soviet Government of Workers and Peasants. [67]

The truth was, however (as Chinese Communist Party statistics admit),
that the Chinese Communist mass movement was undergoing an acute transformation from primarily proletarian to primarily peasant composition.
Near the end of 1926, according to Communist figures, at least 66 percent
of Chinese Communist Party membership could be classed as proletarian.
Another 22 percent were considered to be intellectuals. Only 5 percent were
peasants, and 2 percent were soldiers. [68] But by the early months of 1930,
elements which could possibly be labeled working class totaled only 8 per-

cent of Chinese Communist Party membership, while the number of industrial workers was "still smaller, accounting for only 2%" of Party membership. [69] The Chinese Red Army which, more than any other Red organ, had been responsible for Chinese Communist victories and the establishment of soviets, was overwhelmingly peasant.

This was the Party and this was the military force upon which Moscow depended for the transformation of the agrarian struggle into urban insurrection.

The second Stalinist misconception comprised a faulty evaluation of the Feng, Yen, Wang, and Kwangsi rebellions which were factional struggles rather than deep-seated conflicts capable of being transformed into class wars.

The third misconception on the part of Stalin and his followers was twofold: an overestimation of the "revival of the labor movement" in China as the "most-important, ever-growing symbol of the revolutionary upsurge" and a faulty understanding of labor's relationship to the Chinese Communist Party. For, despite the numerous strikes which Communist officials had so carefully recorded, the Chinese proletariat was not then organized for, nor (if subsequent events are a criterion) politically susceptible to, calls for armed rebellion. The Communist Party, furthermore, had much less influence over the labor movement than it had enjoyed during the peak of labor unrest that characterized the Borodin period. Party nuclei were few and scattered. Party fractions had lost their former power. Even trade-union organizations had "shrunk to almost nothing. "[70]

During the summer of 1930 Li Li-san, translating Comintern policies into a plan for attacks on Changsha, Hankow, and other urban centers, compounded Stalinist strategical errors with tactical mistakes of his own. Chinese Communist forces, enjoying momentary success, captured Changsha in late July and succeeded in holding the city for nearly a week. But with insufficient support from urban masses, Red units were forced to withdraw, and other cities, more heavily garrisoned than Changsha, could not be captured at all. Although Li Li-san pushed his insurrectionary policy throughout the summer, the campaign was a failure, whereupon the Comintern, disturbed by these defeats, dispatched Ch'ü Ch'iu-pai and Chou En-lai (who were in Moscow at the time) to China for the convening of the Third Plenum of the Central Committee of the Chinese Communist Party in Lushan.

The Report of the Third Plenum, drafted by Ch'ü Ch'iu-pai and Chou En-lai, rebuked Li Li-san for having "overestimated the tempo" and for having committed tactical mistakes; nevertheless, it stated that the general line was still "in complete harmony with the Comintern. " The task of the Chinese Communist Party, according to the report, was to consolidate existing but scattered soviet districts, weld them together, strengthen and centralize the leadership of the Red Armies, set broader peasant masses in motion, and establish a Central Soviet Government to develop toward the industrial cities. [71]

Within a few weeks, however, the Comintern on the basis of further Chinese

Communist defeats ordered a complete change of policy, the withdrawal
of Li Li-san from active Party policy making, and the substitution of a new
Party leadership.

Li Li-san's overthrow was directed by the Comintern representative in
China, Pavel Mif, and by a group of recently returned graduates from Sun
Yat-sen University in Moscow. Weeks later Li Li-san, answering for his
failure before the Oriental Department of the Comintern in Moscow, admitted a long series of errors: he had thought that he could mobilize the
working class "simply by raising the slogan of military insurrection"; he
had attempted an insurrectionary policy without proper political preparation;
he had thought that the revolutionary situation was spread evenly throughout China and that a revolutionary government could not be set up until he
had occupied large industrial and administrative cities; he had overestimated the upsurge of the world revolutionary movement; he had maintained
that the victory of the bourgeois democratic revolution would go directly
over into a socialist revolution.

The Comintern, finding Li Li-san guilty of "non-Marxist and non-Leninist
blind actionism," required him to remain in Moscow indefinitely for purposes of Bolshevik study. At the same time, while urging Li to "expose
the whole clique situation" in the Chinese Communist Party, Russian Bolshevik leaders condemned Ch'ü Ch'iu-pai for his actions at the Third Plenum.
Ch'ü Ch'iu-pai, according to Comintern officials, had repudiated the Li
Li-san line before his departure from Moscow prior to the Third Plenum.
Yet, upon his arrival in China, Ch'ü had "double-crossed" the Comintern
by ignoring directives and softening his criticisms of Li Li-san in documents of the Third Plenum. [72]

Of further concern to the Comintern— and one of the more notable findings of the investigation— was the fact that Chinese Communist leaders had
expressed keen resentment over Russian domination within the Red hierarchy.
Chinese comrades, according to Li Li-san, felt that the Russians not only
did not understand conditions in China, but also harbored narrow racial
prejudices. [73]

The "Returned Students": January 1931 – January 1935

From January 1931 until January 1935, nominal leadership of the Chinese
Communist Party— at least partly on Russian advice— rested in the hands
of a group centering on Wang Ming (Ch'en Shao-yü). But this was, in fact,
a critical transition period in the development of the Chinese Communist
Party, a period during which the peasant composition of the Red movement
achieved recognition and during which Mao Tse-tung gradually increased
his power.

As early as 1927 Mao had recognized the peasants as the chief dynamic
force in the Chinese revolution. "If we allot ten points to the accomplish-
ment of the democratic revolution," he wrote in a report on the Hunanese
peasant movement, "then the achievements of the urban dwellers and the
military units rate only three points, while the remaining seven points should

go to the peasants in their rural revolution. " In terms of recent Chinese
Communist attempts at retailoring their ideology more nearly in conformity
with that of the Soviet Union, it is significant that the 1951 Chinese version
of Mao Tse-tung's <u>Collected</u> <u>Works</u> has omitted this statement. Whether
or not it is ever allowed to reappear in official Communist doctrine, this
concept remains fundamental to Mao's political strategy and tactics between
1927 and 1950. According to Mao in 1927, the millions of poor peasants
had nothing to lose by revolt and everything to gain. "Sun Yat-sen devoted
forty years to the national revolution," Mao stated in his report. "What he
wanted but failed to achieve has been accomplished by the peasants in a few
months. "[74]

But Mao did not yet have control of the Chinese Communist movement.
At the Fourth Plenum in January 1931, a group of recently returned students, centering on Wang Ming and supported by Pavel Mif, took over leadership of the Chinese Communist Party. Hsiang Chung-fa, surviving Li
Li-san's dismissal, continued to serve as Secretary General until his execution by the Kuomintang in June 1931, but Wang Ming and his followers
enjoyed Comintern blessing and were considered to be the actual leaders
of the Politburo. After Mao had secured his leadership, however, they
were condemned as "dogmatists" by the Chinese Communists on the basis
of what was called their "pure proletarian line" and for their failure to
unite with the Fukien Rebellion against Chiang Kai-shek in 1934. [75]

Chinese Communist leadership remained young, the average age of four
of these men being twenty-nine years, and in other respects their characteristics did not differ radically from those of previous leaderships. At
least five had received a part of their education in the Soviet Union; one
had studied in France, one in Japan, and one, Chang Wen-t'ien, in the
United States. Three classified their fathers as "Mandarin," "provincial
governor," and "boatman," respectively. Two here called their fathers
"wealthy peasants."

After Hsiang Chung-fa's capture and execution by the Kuomintang in
June 1931, Meng Ch'ing-shu (Mme. Ch'en Shao-yü) was elevated to the Politburo, and her husband, Wang Ming, was made Secretary General.

So far Moscow, in centering its attention upon Central Committee headquarters in Shanghai, had tended to overlook developments which were taking
place under Mao Tse-tung and Chu Te in mountain areas of Kiangsi and
Hunan. But as the Red Army grew in strength and as soviets sprang up in
more and more peasant villages, Comintern leaders began gradually to
shift emphasis in the direction of rural areas.

In April 1931 Manuilsky laid down three objectives for the current stage
of the Chinese revolution: the Red Army must be converted into a regular
workers' and peasants' Red Army with a sound territorial base; the economic
and political struggles of the working class and peasantry in nonsoviet territories must be developed through trade-unions, peasant committees, and
propaganda work in various militarist armies; and a central Soviet Government must be formed in China[76] in order to carry out a program of anti-
imperialist and agrarian revolt. [77]

During November 1931, two months after Japanese action in Manchuria, the First All-China Congress of Soviets, meeting in Juichin, established a Chinese Soviet Republic with Mao Tse-tung as chairman and Chang Kuo-t'ao and Hsiang Ying as vice-chairmen. Before adjourning, the Congress accepted a government constitution, passed agrarian and labor laws, and elected a government Central Committee under Mao's chairmanship. In February 1932 the new government declared war on Japan and sent out a call to all classes and political groups in China to join in resisting Japanese aggression. [78] This was the beginning of what was called "a united front from below."

For another year the Central Committee of the Chinese Communist Party maintained its headquarters in Shanghai, while Mao and his followers devoted themselves to affairs of the Juichin Republic, to the building of the Red Army, and to resisting a series of Nationalist attacks which Chiang Kai-shek had initiated. But during the autumn of 1932 Wang Ming, Chang Wen-t'ien, Po Ku (Ch'in Pang-hsien), Shen Tse-min, and other Central Committeemen, under Kuomintang pressure, moved to Juichin. Shortly thereafter Wang Ming was relieved of his position as Secretary General and recalled to the Soviet Union, where he served from 1932 to 1938 as a Chinese Communist representative in Moscow. One is tempted to conclude that this may have been the result of some internal party conflict, but Chang Kuo-t'ao told the author in a personal interview that the Chinese Communist Party was having trouble with its underground apparatus at the time, that someone had to be sent to Moscow, and that Wang Ming seemed the logical one. [79] He was replaced as Secretary General by Po Ku (Ch'in Pang-hsien). [80]

The necessity for meeting Chiang Kai-shek's attacks was undoubtedly a positive factor in the long-range growth and strengthening of the Red Army, in the consolidation of Mao's power within the Party, and in the eventual expansion of the Communist Party itself. But the immediate effect of Chiang's campaigns was to weaken the Soviet Republic and to force it out of Kiangsi.

Chiang's first offensive, undertaken in December 1930, proved unsuccessful. Red leaders, with their forces centered in mountain areas, found the terrain well suited for guerrilla warfare. Basic to Communist tactics was the principle that Red troops should attack only when they enjoyed local superiority over the enemy and were certain to win a restricted engagement. In order to create such situations, therefore, Mao and Chu Te had trained their troops in tricks of decoy and ambush designed to isolate small Nationalist detachments from the main body. The theory was that, once this maneuver had been accomplished, it would be comparatively easy to surround and annihilate the enemy unit and make away with their weapons and supplies. [81]

During May and June 1931 Chiang Kai-shek pressed his second attack. This time he dispatched 200,000 men (nearly double the number employed in the first offensive) under Ho Ying-ch'in, while Communist leaders made what preparations they could with the aid of arms and equipment captured during the previous offensive.

Ho's plan was to advance slowly, consolidating his gains as he moved along. But Red troops, attacking the Nationalist rear, were able to repulse the Kuomintang attack in fifteen days and, according to Chu Te, to capture 30,000 rifles.

Chiang took personal command of the third campaign, which lasted from July to October 1931. This time, according to Chu Te, Red Leaders miscalculated, being unaware that Chiang was so soon in a position to strike again. Nationalist troops advanced along four parallel lines, concentrating their attack upon soviets in Kiangsi. To meet this offensive, Communist elements infiltrated the spaces between Chiang's lines and began harassing operations. Since the weather was hot, Nationalist troops, allegedly less accustomed to hard marching than the Reds, soon began to tire, and as a result, Communist tactics were momentarily successful. Neither side was able to register a decisive victory, however, and the campaign came to a conclusion only when Chiang, as a result of the Mukden incident, was forced to withdraw his troops. In order to avoid further stalemates, Chiang next made plans for co-ordinated military offensives and economic blockade. Nationalist leaders laid out a whole network of blockhouses and field fortifications to isolate Communist territories and began, at the same time, the mobilization of a million men.

The combined military and economic attack which Chiang subsequently loosed upon the Soviet areas was already endangering Juichin when the Second Congress of Chinese Soviets opened in January 1934. At the Fifth Plenum of the Chinese Communist Party, held concurrently, another of the "returned student" group, Chang Wen-t'ien, replaced Po Ku as Secretary General of the Party. Chang Kuo-t'ao reports that at the Fifth Plenum Po Ku attacked Mao for his "countryside policy" and "banditry doctrine" and used every effort to keep Mao's growing power in bounds. [82] But Mao seems to have dominated the Second Congress of Soviets. Admitting the serious effects of Chiang Kai-shek's blockade, Mao called for an aggressive program to save the Soviet Republic and to enlarge it in the face of the Nationalist offensive. He wanted to build Red Army strength to a million men, to increase the size of reserve units such as the Red Guards and the Communist Youth Guards, and to boost production, both agricultural and industrial.

But during the Congress, Nationalist forces were already tightening their encirclement of soviet areas. Hard fighting took place during the spring and summer of 1934, and casualties mounted on both sides. According to Mao and Chu Te, the Nationalists maneuvered Red forces into abandoning their guerrilla tactics in favor of positional warfare and thus gained a further advantage. [83]

Before the year was up, Communist leaders found themselves compelled to organize a nearly complete evacuation of soviet areas and a retreat from their strongholds in Central China. By the date of the Juichin Republic's fall (November 10, 1934), they and their followers were already embarking upon the Long March, which, during the following twelve months, took them more than 6,000 miles across the face of China.

The Fourth Period of Leadership

This stage, which began in August 1935, saw the completion of the Long March, the establishment of a united front against Japan, victory in the civil war against Chiang Kai-shek and the Kuomintang, the establishment of a nationwide, Communist-controlled People's Republic, and the concurrent maturing of present Party leadership under Mao Tse-tung.

It is difficult to obtain details concerning Mao Tse-tung's actual achievement of power within the Chinese Communist Party. The following analysis depends rather heavily upon information given the author by Chang Kuo-t'ao, who, throughout the Long March and for two years thereafter, was Mao's chief rival for power. For the most part, Chang's statements are supported by the fragmentary documentary evidence, but he himself emphasized that he had no notes or documents for reference and was, furthermore, a party to the controversy he was describing. [84]

Chang Kuo-t'ao states that Mao's power dates from the Tsun-yi Conference in Kweichow during January 1935. Prior to that, Mao's position in the Party was considered relatively unimportant, Chang insists, both because Moscow had favored the "returned students" and because of Po Ku's attacks on Mao's "countryside" policies.

Sometime in late October or November 1934, according to Chang, Communist authorities in Juichin received a radiogram from Moscow advising them to pull out and seek safety, perhaps as far away as Outer Mongolia. The local decision to begin the Long March was made by Po Ku and Chou En-lai. The evacuation began November 10, and, for a number of months thereafter, Communist leaders had no contact with Moscow.

At Tsun-yi various Communist leaders attacked Po Ku and succeeded in removing him from power. Mao and his supporters based their attack on the charges that Po Ku had used ineffective guerrilla tactics against the Kuomintang and had weakened the Communist position by refusing to co-operate with an anti-Kuomintang revolt in Fukien during 1933. Chang Kuo-t'ao, who was not present at the meeting, but who kept in touch by telegram, went further, attacking the whole principle of soviets for China.

The conference upheld the first two charges, but refused to support Chang's attack on the soviet principle. As a result of these debates, Mao achieved power, while Chang assumed the role of an oppositionist. In June 1935 the main column of the Long March made a junction in Szechwan Province with troops of Chang Kuo-t'ao and Hsu Hsiang-ch'ien, who had set up a soviet base in this area a short time previously. After proceeding to Mao-erh-kai, the two groups held a joint meeting where the differences between Mao and Chang broke into open debate.

The conflict arose over ratification of the decisions reached at Tsun-yi, Chang reopening his argument that the soviet principle was inapplicable to Chinese conditions. Beyond this, a further disagreement developed over the ultimate destination of the Long March. All admitted that a period of rest was necessary, but Mao wanted to settle somewhere near Inner Mongolia, perhaps in the vicinity of Ningsia, and as close as possible to the troops of Kao Kang, a peasant guerrilla leader who had participated in building a soviet in Shensi. Chang Kuo-t'ao, on the other hand, proposed to continue into Sinkiang.

At this point, according to Chang, contact was momentarily re-established with Moscow, whereupon the Comintern proposed the recognition of two independent bases, one under Mao, the other under Chang—a solution to which the Chinese could not agree. Thereupon, Moscow sent Lin Piao's uncle, Lin Yü-yin, to take over authority and seek some other way out; this attempt also failed to win Chinese support.

Chang maintains that Moscow then approved the journey to Sinkiang and that the two groups, having separated, made another juncture and began a crossing of the Yellow River. Kuomintang forces interposed, however, and nearly destroyed two Communist armies. A conflicting source maintains that, after the second juncture of the two forces, the old conflict broke out again, whereupon Chang and Hsu returned to Mao-erh-kai, whence they struck westward into Sikang, while Mao proceeded to Shensi. [85] In any case, the two groups both settled in Shensi eventually, for it was there that the final Mao-Chang clash took place.

Mao and his followers selected Pao An as their capital, remaining there until December 1936, when, after the Communist capture of Yenan, they transferred their headquarters to the latter town. The period from the termination of the Long March until the summer of 1937 was one of negotiations which were characteristic of a new tactical stage in Chinese Communist development.

The Japanese invasion of Manchuria had been recognized by Russian and Chinese Communist leaders alike as a particularly critical development. In Moscow, Bolshevik strategists saw not only a new imperialist threat to the Chinese revolution, but also a new menace to the Soviet Union, which, during the progress of the Five Year Plan, was especially anxious to preserve world peace. In China, Mao and his followers, beyond their awareness of these factors, may have seen the further probability that unified Chinese action against Japan would bring an end to the anti-Communist "extermination campaigns" of Chiang Kai-shek.

As early as April 1932 the Chinese Communists had "called upon the mass of Chinese people to join . . . in the fight against Japanese imperialism," and in January 1933 a Comintern publication carried a similar appeal on the part of the Chinese Soviet Government and the Revolutionary War Council of the Chinese Red Army signed by Mao, Chang Kuo-t'ao, Chu Te, and others:

> . . . We declare before the whole Chinese people: The Red Army is prepared to enter into a fighting alliance with any army or any body of troops against the Japanese invasion. Our conditions for such alliance are: (1) immediate cessation of the offensive against the Soviet districts; (2) immediate granting of democratic popular rights, the right of combination, freedom of speech and press,

the right to hold meetings, etc.; (3) immediate arming of the people and formation of armed volunteer troops for the fight for the
defense of the independence and unity of China . . . [86]

On August 1, 1935, the Mao-erh-kai Conference in northwestern Szechwan
decided on an anti-Japanese People's United Front and issued a proclamation
urging all classes to fight against Japan. Calling on "all fellow countrymen,
in spite of differences of political opinions, strivings, and interests" to
"unite as one man," the Convention made a special appeal to Chiang Kai-
shek, promising to co-operate with the Kuomintang if Chiang would stop
his fight "against his own people." At the same time the proclamation
called also for the "formation of a United All-Chinese People's Government
of National Defence jointly with the Soviet Government and the Anti-Japanese
local authorities in Manchuria" and for the "organization of a united All-
China Anti-Japanese Army jointly with the Red Army and the Anti-Japanese
partisan units in Manchuria."[87]

On the following day, August 2, Georgi Dimitrov, advocating a world-
wide united front policy to the Seventh Congress of the Communist International in Moscow, said:

> . . . We therefore approve the initiative take by our courageous
> brother Party of China in the creation of a most extensive anti-
> imperialist united front against Japanese imperialism and its
> Chinese agents, jointly with all those organized forces existing
> on the territory of China who are ready to wage a real struggle
> for the salvation of their country and their people. [88]

Five days later Wang Ming told the same Congress:

> In my opinion and in the opinion of the entire Central Committee
> of the Communist Party of China, the latter, together with the
> Soviet government of China should issue a joint appeal to the
> whole nation, to all parties, groups, troops, mass organizations,
> and all prominent political and social persons, to organize together
> with us an all-China united people's government of national de-
> fence. [89]

Chang Kuo-t'ao states that to his knowledge the Chinese Communists,
prior to the Seventh Congress, had carried on no communications with
Moscow in regard to a broad united-front policy as opposed to the old
"united front from below."[90] It is also worth noting that at the Congress
Chinese delegates other than Wang Ming were continuing to call for an
anti-imperialist and anti-Kuomintang united front as late as August 11—,
nine days after Dimitrov's speech.[91] Both Chinese and Russian leaders,
according to Chang Kuo-t'ao, had been considering the problem of opposing
Japanese expansion and, independently, had reached some of the same conclusions concerning a broad united front. There was no co-ordination, however, until Lin Yü-ying returned to China with a copy of the Seventh Congress
Resolution dealing with the new united-front policy.[92]

This resolution, passed August 20, demanded a broad front in colonial and semicolonial countries, including China, "under the slogan of a national-revolutionary struggle of the armed people against the imperialist enslavers, in the first place against Japanese imperialism and its Chinese servitors."[93] In China the soviets were to be the rallying center of this movement, but by implication the road was left open for the Kuomintang if Chiang saw fit to call off his anti-Communist campaigns and join in the fight against Japan.

Chiang showed no willingness to heed Communist appeals until his kidnaping at Sian in December 1936. At this time Chang Hsüeh-liang, whose forces had been driven out of Manchuria into Shensi, and Yang Hü-cheng, the Pacification Commissioner of Shensi, captured Chiang and pressed upon him the view that the main war was against the Japanese, rather than the Communists. In the negotiations which led to Chiang's eventual release, Chinese Communist leaders acted as mediators, a service which paved the way for effecting a Communist-Kuomintang truce. This took place shortly after Chiang's return to Nanking.

Six months later the Chinese Communists offered specifically to abolish soviets and the Red Army designation, to carry out "democracy", to abandon its policy of overthrowing the Kuomintang, and to discontinue land confiscations in return for a Kuomintang cessation of the civil war, a Kuomintang policy of "democracy and freedom," the convocation of a National Assembly, concrete preparations for war against Japan, and an improvement in the people's livelihood.[94]

The Kuomintang took no action in regard to this offer, but negotiations continued between the two parties. In the meantime, Japanese expansion on the Asian mainland was giving rise to militant Chinese nationalism and widespread demands for unity. With the beginning of the Sino-Japanese War in July 1937, an agreement was finally reached. Communist leaders issued statements to the effect that the first step in preparation for a Marxist socialist state was now believed to be the attainment of national independence and of "democratic" institutions and that further Communist action toward the attainment of these goals would coincide with the Three Principles of Dr. Sun Yat-sen.[95]

Relations between Red Army and peasantry were necessarily revised. For whereas under the soviets Communist military forces had been expanded at the expense of landowning and similar sections of the populace, united-front policies forbade the antagonizing of gentry and related classes. During the uneasy Communist-Kuomintang alliance which resulted from the conclusion of these agreements, Mao's leadership was subjected to another internal crisis.

In translating Dimitrov's united front policy into Chinese terms, Mao advanced the slogan, "Defeat for all!" meaning defeat for the Japanese and eventual defeat for non-Communist groups in the alliance, including the Kuomintang. Attacking this policy, Chang Kuo-t'ao proposed the slogan, "Victory for all!" with the hope that, through a sincere alliance, the Communists might be able to lead the Kuomintang and other non–Communist groups along a more progressive path than they had followed in the past. The two policies were debated at a conference at Lochuan, but when it became clear (according to Chang) that a majority of those present favored a "Victory for all!" policy, Mao cut off further discussion and closed the meeting. [96] The issue was then referred to the Comintern, which decided in favor of Mao. Moscow endorsed a Chinese Communist charge that Chang had "betrayed" Communism and "the cause of the anti-Japanese front" by being too friendly with the Kuomintang and confirmed his expulsion from the Party. [97]

In prosecuting Mao's "defeat for all" united-front policy, Chinese Communist leaders, while championing the cause of the peasant, made what use they could of their uneasy alliance with the Kuomintang. Then, once the war was over, they proceeded to exploit Kuomintang weaknesses, leading armies of dissatisfied peasants against the Nationalist government. The results were military victories for Mao and the establishment in late September 1949 of a Chinese People's Republic.

During the Japanese War the Chinese Communist Party strengthened itself both organizationally and ideologically. Much of its organizational experience took place in the so-called liberated areas behind Japanese lines, and it was in these areas that Red leaders — especially the young ones — became expert in guerrilla warfare, propaganda techniques, and civil organization. [98]

Ideologically, the chief development during the Japanese War was the completion of Mao Tse-tung's blueprint for the New Democracy. To a large extent, Mao's concept had been derived from Lenin's "Theses on the National and Colonial Questions," presented to the Second Congress of the Communist International in 1920, and from the "Theses on the Revolutionary Movement in the Colonies and Semi-Colonies," passed by the Sixth Congress in 1928. Mao, therefore, in adjusting these principles to his own revolutionary experiences and to social and economic peculiarities of the Chinese situation, produced a plan which differed in detail from programs of the past but which found a logical position within the dialectics of the Leninist-Stalinist revolutionary system.

> The thesis that the state form is the dictatorship of all revolutionary classes and the government form is the system of democratic centralism is the political foundation of the "new democracy" . . . [99]

In an economic sense, Mao's program amounts to a Communist elaboration of Dr. Sun Yat-sen's plan for state control of distribution, transportation, and production as a weapon against imperialism. For the present it contemplates a mixed economy undertaken partly by co-operatives, partly by private enterprise, and partly by the state. Being a Communist concept, however, the New Democracy must be considered as only one stage in a planned and, from the Communist standpoint, an inevitable advance into Marxist socialism and communism.

That Mao did not have any intention of ignoring Communist teachings or of breaching Communist discipline is suggested by the ideological training program which he set in motion during the first months of 1942.[100] Calling together several thousands of Red officials, Mao started them off on a rigorous course in Communist philosophy, strategy, and tactics based upon a textbook of twenty-two outstanding Communist documents. Both Chinese and Western Communist selections were included, but both proportion and sequence gave emphasis to Mao's writings and to those of other CCP writers, rather than to the writings of Marx, Engels, Lenin, and Stalin. It should not be overlooked, however, that the Chinese writers developed their arguments within a Bolshevik framework and relied heavily upon Marx, Engels, Lenin, and Stalin for their supporting citations.

When these thousands of Red officials had completed this indoctrination, Mao dispersed them throughout Red areas of China in order to instruct the rank and file and, at the same time, to tighten up the Communist Party apparatus. Mao used this opportunity to expel undesirable elements from the Party hierarchy, but certain men (like Wang Ming) who had been named as purge victims in National Central News Agency reports were as recently as 1948 occupying official, if somewhat subordinate, positions within the top hierarchy of the Chinese Communist Party.[101]

Over-all Trends

From 1921 through 1931 Moscow was responsible for making and breaking top Chinese Communist leadership. In the beginning, it is true, Ch'en Tu-hsiu achieved leadership through his own initiative, prestige and organizational efforts. But after the First Congress, he remained in office only through sufferance on the part of Moscow. This does not mean that the Chinese subordinated themselves gracefully. On the contrary, there is evidence that many of them resented Russian interference and were sometimes outspoken about it. But during these years they either submitted to discipline or were relieved of their responsibilities by the hierarchy.

Between 1928 and 1934, however, the composition of the Chinese Communist Party underwent a radical change. Proletarian membership nearly disappeared while peasants flocked into the ranks. Mao sensed and made the most of this trend from the beginning, transforming theory into agrarian revolutionary practice (Mao has also won recognition as a theorist), but Moscow was slow to recognize what was taking place. As a result, Mao and his associates, blessed with an opportunity accorded by circumstances to few Communist leaders in recent years, rose to power largely through their own efforts and this fact, combined with conditions pertaining to the Juichin Republic and the Long March, established new criteria for leadership.

Moscow's blessing continued, no doubt, to be desirable, but on-the-scene performance in China became increasingly more important than close relationships with Comintern agents such as Heinz Neumann and Pavel Mif.

For during the Long March and the Japanese War a prospective Chinese
Communist leader, even if approved by Moscow, had yet to win his position
through endurance, personal magnetism, guerrilla leadership, administrative excellence, propaganda activities, or organizational work among the
peasantry. He had to be tough; he had to command respect; he had to be
able.

Yet the hierarchy in which he rose was by no means democratic in the
Western sense. Behavior was governed by the principles of democratic
centralism, a disciplinary system requiring rigid personal subordination
to the will of the majority (or, in cases, to the will of the superior hierarchy). At intervals there have been intensive campaigns— some carried
on through intervention from Moscow, others initiated by Chinese leadership, including Mao himself— to rid the party of deviationists, incompe-
tents, and other elements considered undesirable by those in power.

At various points during the course of Chinese Communist Party history,
internal conflicts have found expression in clique activities which were
serious enough to cause concern in Moscow. Up to this writing, however,
there is no reliable evidence that these personal struggles (or official
campaigns for weeding out undesirables) have ever led to disappearances,
assassinations, or executions on the scale common to the Soviet Union
after 1934. In this respect, Chinese Communist practice is like that characteristic of Russia during the earlier years of the Soviet regime. Chinese
Communist leaders have risen and fallen; some have been reprimanded;
others have been expelled; thousands have been killed by Nationalist armies
and Nationalist police, and thousands of non-Communists have been killed
by Communist armies and police. But to date there is no authenticated
record of a prominent Chinese Communist leader executed by his own Party,
no matter how serious the doctrinal deviation. On the contrary, there has
been a strong tendency— best evidenced in the case of Li Li-san— to reform
the fallen leader and even to give him limited opportunities for reconstruct-
ing his career.

The current internal political health of the Chinese Communist Party is
uncertain. There have been reports of antagonistic clique alignments, both
on the basis of personal conflicts and on the basis of individual attitudes
toward the Soviet Union. But there is also a respectable body of contrary
evidence which would suggest that high-level internal conflicts may be at a
minimum, that discipline is strict, and that Mao's position is generally respected throughout the Party.

With the development of the Korean War, and especially during the early
months of 1952, the Chinese Communist Party has carried on an intensive
campaign against "corruption, decay, and bureaucracy" in both Party and
non-Party ranks. There are evidences indicating that the purpose of this
campaign is threefold: to insure cleaner and more efficient government; to
promote class struggle against groups considered inimicable to Bolshevik
interests at this particular stage of the revolution; and to cleanse the Party
of undesirable personnel. The seriousness of Communist intent can be

judged from remarks made by Kao Kang in a Report at the Higher-level Cadres Meeting of the Northeast Bureau of the Central Committee of the Chinese Communist Party, January 10, 1952:

The following should be accomplished during the present campaign:

(1) Purge all departments of corruption, waste and bureaucracy. The cases of corruption and waste should be given penalties ranging from dismissal, prison terms, labor reform to death sentence. [102]

IV. THE SOCIAL CHARACTERISTICS OF CHINESE PARTY ELITES

For the greater part of three decades the Kuomintang and the Communist Party have fought one another with all the bitterness of a class war. On the surface the rival interests involved in this conflict seem clear, for here are all the superficial characteristics of a struggle between masses on the one hand and classes on the other. The policies of the Kuomintang and the way of life of its leaders have again and again lent credence to the picture which its enemies propagate, namely, that the Kuomintang is simply a landlord clique. Moreover, the utilization by the Communists of peasant discontent, together with their insistent profession of a Marxian ideology, has created the strong impression that their movement is a movement of the masses. But an examination of membership data raises the question: how far does the character of Kuomintang and Communist leaderships support or contradict these preconceptions?

It is certainly true that Communist Party leaders differ from Kuomintang leaders in social and economic background. Indeed, the leaders of the right, center, and left within the Kuomintang also differ in these respects. But before considering these differences, we ought to take into account a number of rather striking similarities. For despite all the detailed differences, we find ourselves forced to concede that a major portion of the elite of both movements came from quite similar high social strata, and responded to similar Western and native influences during their years of growth and education.

Common Characteristics

In both parties, the leaders have been drawn most frequently from a relatively thin upper layer of the Chinese population. In both parties these men were often the sons of landlords, merchants, scholars, or officials, and they usually came from parts of China where Western influence had first penetrated and where the penetration itself was most vigorous. All of them had higher educations, and most of them had studied abroad. The leaders of both parties, despite a relatively high status in private life, showed a reluctance or perhaps an inability to establish private careers. The majority were alienated intellectuals, men and women whose Western educations isolated them from the main currents of Chinese society. In the chaos of modern China, these persons became full-time professional politicians specializing, for the most part, in military violence or in party administration. Whichever party they belonged to, Communist or Kuomintang, they differed from the imperial elite, which we described at the beginning of this study (cf. pp. 1 – 2), in that they were drawn from a much wider circle. It is true that the sons of scholar-officials continued to enter politics — and very successfully — but more noteworthy, perhaps, is the fact that recent revolutions in China have brought forward the sons of the nouveau-riche compradors, other business classes of coastal cities, the sons of landlords, and recently, even, the sons of wealthy peasants. On the other hand, despite plebeian protesta-

46

tions of the Communists, the relatively smaller mass of proletarians have continued to enjoy only limited access to the elite.

The basic similarity in social origins of the largest portion of both Kuomintang and Communist leaders is emphasized by figures on their fathers' occupations and social status (cf. Table 2). The 1945 Central

TABLE 2. FATHER'S GENERAL OCCUPATION

	Kuomintang CECs 1924, 1926, 1929		Communist Politburo		Communist CEC 1945	
	No.	Percent	No.	Percent	No.	Percent
Wealthy landlord or scholar landlord	10	21.3	3	12.5	7	23.3
Scholar-official	3	6.4	4	16.7	3	10.0
Scholar	3	6.4	1	4.2	—	——
Merchant-scholar or wealthy merchant	7	14.9	—	——	1	3.3
Upper class, indeterminate	—	——	—	——	1	3.3
		48.9		33.3		40.0
Other landlords	4	8.5	2	8.3	1	3.3
Other merchants	15	31.9	2	8.3	1	3.3
Professional revolutionary	2	4.3	—	——	—	——
Wealthy peasant	—	——	6	25.0	6	20.0
Middle class, indeterminate	—	——	—	——	3	10.0
		44.7		41.7		36.7
Other peasants	3	6.4	4	16.7	5	16.7
Workers	—	——	2	8.3	2	6.7
		6.4		25.0		23.3
Total known	47	100.0	24	100.0	30	100.0
Don't know	23		18		14	
Total	70		42		44	

*For full data see Appendix D.

Committee of the Chinese Communist Party contained eight sons of landlords, two sons of merchants, and one son of an official. Against these eleven men of high social status, there were also eleven sons of peasants, of whom six were wealthy peasants. There were also two sons of workers. And the composition of the Politburos from the beginning until 1945 was similar. For these ten leading bodies (including, as in all our Politburo tabulations, the First Congress in 1921 and the "ruling clique" of August

1927) contained, in all, five sons of landlords, two sons of merchants, four sons of officials, and one son of a scholar. Against these twelve men of upper-class origin, there were ten sons of peasants, of whom six were wealthy peasants. There were also two sons of workers. Thus we find about half of the Communist elite drawn from upper-class and middle-class families, and another quarter from the prosperous section of the peasantry.

In the Kuomintang elite all but three of the fifty-one members of the first three Central Executive Committees whose occupations we know were upper or upper-middle class. Aside from these three (all sons of medium or poor peasants), there were fourteen sons of landlords, three sons of officials, and three sons of scholars whose occupations we cannot further identify. In addition there were twenty-two sons of merchants who, although middle class, enjoyed less prestige than would merchants in the West.

In this and some later tabulations we include only the first three commit-tees because the informants who provided the data had enjoyed close contacts with earlier, rather than later, members of the Kuomintang.

It is not easy to secure material concerning the social and economic status of Chinese leaders. They have been traditionally reticent about revealing information on the source or level of an individual's income. Moreover, many leaders, especially among the Communists, lived underground for many years at a stretch, assumed revolutionary names, and covered their movements with utmost caution. Nevertheless, a few broad conclusions can be drawn from the reports of Western businessmen, missionaries, and travelers who succeeded in establishing close personal relationships with influential Chinese. Such informants have materially aided this study by reporting on Chinese leaders they have known, providing information on source of income and occupation of father, and offering subjective ratings of financial status. The resultant data on Politburo members have been rela-tively full, owing to the fact that members of this body are few in number.

On the basis of these data it is clear that both elites have drawn heavily from limited circles of the population. There may be support for the im-pression that the social origins of Kuomintang leaders were higher than those of the Communist elite, but three cautions must be observed. Note first that many of the middle-class Kuomintang leaders were merchants' sons, of limited social status. Second, note the large number of "don't knows." For about one-third of the members of the first three Kuomin-tang CEC's and for over 40 percent of the CCP Politburo members we do not know the fathers' occupations, and there is no ground for assuming that these men had the same backgrounds as did those whose status we know. Usu-ally, leaders whose origins are unreported in biographical sources are those of lower-class origins; prominent parents are likely to be known. This generali-zation certainly applies to Kuomintang leaders, for their ideology is such that they normally prefer to publicize reputable origins. With Communists, however, the pattern is quite the opposite, both in China and elsewhere. They prefer to hide upper-class backgrounds and to feature or even fabricate proletarian origins. Thus, among the Communist "don't knows" there is probably a higher proportion of upper-class parents than among Kuomintang "don't knows." This is one reason for suspecting that the relatively small difference in the social status of fathers of Kuomintang and Communist leaders is not significant.

A third factor also tends to emphasize the fallacy in assuming that Kuomintang leaders came from higher social backgrounds than Communist leaders. Since our data ran out after 1929, we used Kuomintang CEC's only through that date. If we limit our examination to Politburos appointed up to and through that same year, we find that only three of the Politburo members were sons of peasants and that only one member was the son of a proletarian, while eight were sons of upper-class or middle-class parents. Clearly, then, in both the Communist Party and the Kuomintang the plebeians entered later. This is not to deny the possibility, of course, that there may have been a genuine difference between parties in the number of plebeians. The point to be noted, however, is that both parties drew heavily on the upper ranks of the population for recruiting their leadership

TABLE 3. STATUS OF FATHERS OF POLITBUROCRATS
(Showing Entry of Plebeians After 1927)

Politburo	Upper and Middle	Lower
1921	4	—
April 1, 1927	4	1
July 13, 1927	4	—
August 1927	3	2
1928	3	2
January 1931	4	1
June 1931	4	—
1934	7	3
1937	5	2
1945	9	3

(cf. Table 3). It is not at all surprising that the Kuomintang included in its leadership a number of persons born to wealth and prominence, but it is worthy of note that among Communist leaders, too, we find, for example, three fathers who were wealthy landlords, one who was both a wealthy landlord and an official, and in addition to these, three men who listed their fathers respectively as statesman, Mandarin, and provincial governor.

So, too, members of the two elites are similar in the educations they have received. Aside from two members of the Politburo and one other member of the 1945 Central Committee of the Communist Party, all the elite members on whom we have information enjoyed a higher education (cf. Table 4). Some went to universities in China or abroad, some had classical Chinese educations, some attended military schools; but, with the rarest exceptions, they were trained men. Despite the revolutionary character of recent Chinese history, political involvement did not truncate their education as it did in the cases of so many Soviet and Nazi leaders. Despite the poverty of China and the very small proportion of families able to afford higher educations for their sons, leaders simply did not arise by making their own way through channels outside normal educational patterns.

TABLE 4. EDUCATION OF ELITE MEMBERS

	Kuomintang CEC	Politburo
No higher education	2	2
Chinese education only	123	2
Foreign education	136	25
Total known	261	29
Don't know	26	13
Total	287	42

Once touched by an education, the hitherto fatalistic peasant boy who has looked forward to a life no different from that of his ancestors gradually achieves a consciousness of progress and an awareness of the good things which technology can provide. And whatever his local background, the man trained as an engineer is impressed by the fact that in his own country the number of factories, and hence of jobs, is limited, with foreign "imperialists" filling most of the top positions of a technical nature. Soon he concludes that, born in the West, he would have a job and command a factory, but that, short of a thoroughgoing revolution, he can look forward to no better prospect than unemployment in his own backward country. So, too, the man trained as a banker or chemist feels a similar lack of opportunities in his field. So it is for these and innumerable other reasons, some of them exceedingly subtle and complex, that students tended to provide the leadership for both Communist and "bourgeois nationalist" movements.

The impact of Western thought upon such people has provided fuel for anti-Western movements. This impact on both Kuomintang and Communist elites is indicated by figures showing the geographical distribution of institutions which have provided elite members with their educations. In the case of each elite the majority have been educated abroad. Out of 261 Kuomintang CEC members whose educational careers we know, 138 were educated abroad, and out of 29 Politburo members whose educational careers we know, 25 were educated abroad. Russian training accounts for the higher proportion of foreign training among Communist leaders, but if we leave

TABLE 5. UNIVERSITIES ATTENDED*

| | Kuomintang CEC | | | Politburo | | Communist CEC | |
	No.	Percent		No.	Percent	No.	Percent
Chinese university	86	33.0					
Chinese military school	88	33.7	China	13	44.8	23	54.8
Chinese classical education	15	5.7					
Japanese university	42	16.1					
Japanese military school	26	10.0	Japan	5	17.2	5	11.9
United States	40	15.3		2	6.9	1	2.4
France	13	5.0		6	20.7	12	28.6
Germany	13	5.0		2	6.9	3	7.1
Great Britain	15	5.7		—	——	—	——
Belgium	2	.8		—	——	1	2.4
Soviet Union	14	5.4		20	69.0	25	59.5
Other	3	1.1		—	——	—	——
None	2	.8		2	6.9	3	7.1
Total known	261	100.0		29	100.0	42	100.0
Don't know	26			13		2	
Total	287			42		44	

*This table is nonadditive since the same individual may go to several universities.

Russian education aside, we still find that 38 percent of the leaders of the Communist Party had been trained in advanced capitalist countries.

As awareness of the role of students might lead us to expect, the leaderships of both Kuomintang and Communist Party were young. Not only did these revolutionists join the movements in their student years, but they rose to positions of leadership fast. Both elites tended to age over the years, but until 1945 no Kuomintang CEC had an average age of over forty-five and no Politburo had an average age over forty (cf. Table 6 for full figures). From 1921 through 1931 in fact the average of each Politburo ranged between twenty-seven and thirty-three, while that of each Kuomintang CEC was either forty-two or forty-three. After that the average ages of both groups started to rise till in 1945 it was forty-nine for the Politburo and fifty-one for Kuomintang CEC. Even these figures are a little low as compared to those for other elites reported in the Hoover Institute Studies, but they are in the usual range. It is only in times of revolutionary change, however, that one finds an elite whose average age is in the thirties or early forties. In a stable society political leadership is likely to be a function of achieved status. "Notables" (to use Max Weber's term) from

TABLE 6. AVERAGE AGES OF PARTY ELITES

Kuomintang CEC	Average Age of Members
1924	43.3
1926	44.6
1929	43.8
1931	42.6
1935	48.9
1945	54.9
Communist Politburo	
1921	29.4
April 1927	33.4
July 1927	27.3
August 1927	29.0
1928	30.0
January 1931	29.0
June 1931	28.4
1934	35.2
1937	39.3
1945	48.9
Communist Party CC, 1945	46.8

other fields of life are recruited to give prestige and standing to the political machines. A political elite of notables is necessarily of reasonable advanced age— usually averaging in the fifties. An exception is the elite in an aristocratic society where a person may be a notable from birth. In such a society, however, he is likely to remain in politics till a fairly advanced age; so the average, although lower than in a democratic society where all must work their way up, is still apt to be well up in the forties. Modern China has certainly not been an aristocratic society in that sense. Neither the Kuomintang nor Communist elites have been born to their positions. They have achieved them by effort, but in the revolutionary conditions that existed they could achieve them rapidly by going directly into politics without establishing an outside reputation first.

As a matter of fact, we find that few of the leaders of either Kuomintang or Communist Party had extrapolitical careers. The overwhelming majority were professional politicians who devoted most of their adult life to party struggles. This we expect to be true of a Communist Politburo. A Politburo member must conform to the Leninist ideal of a professional revolutionary. Following the Politburo pattern in this respect, the 1945 Central Committee of the Communist Party consisted also of professional revolutionists. Forty-five percent made their careers in Party organization; another 39 percent made careers of the army. Thus 84 percent were professionally engaged in revolutionary struggle. Most of the remainder of the CC were presented as coming directly from the work benches. Any large Communist body is required to have some such proletarians as showpieces. How many of them in reality were primarily laborers and how many were primarily Communist functionaries is impossible to say, but even if all five were primarily laborers they were still but a sprinkling. In addition to these persons there were one educator and one journalist, and no persons with any other major career. Thus the Central Committee, like the Politburo, was clearly a body of professional Party activists.

TABLE 7. CAREERS OF 1945 COMMUNIST CENTRAL COMMITTEE MEMBERS

	Number	Percent
Party organization and administration	20	45. 5
Military	17	38. 6
Labor	5	11. 4
Education	1	2. 3
Journalism	1	2. 3
Total	44	100. 0

What is surprising is that the situation was almost identical in the Kuomintang. Fifty-one percent of all Kuomintang CEC members made their careers in Party organization. Thirty-six percent had military careers. Thus 86 percent were above all, professional politicians. Of the residue

TABLE 8. CAREERS OF KUOMINTANG EXECUTIVE COMMITTEEMEN
(In Percents)

	1924	1926	1929	1931	1935	1945	All CEC Members
Organization and administration	58. 3	55. 6	55. 6	63. 9	45. 4	50. 2	50. 5
Military	25. 0	25. 0	41. 7	33. 3	42. 9	37. 2	35. 9
Education	4. 2	5. 6	——	——	5. 0	6. 3	5. 6
Journalism	4. 2	2. 8	2. 8	2. 8	2. 5	3. 1	2. 8
Other	4. 2	2. 8	——	——	1. 7	1. 8	2. 1
Don't know	4. 2	8. 3	——	——	2. 5	1. 4	3. 1
Total	100. 0 (24)	100. 0 (36)	100. 0 (36)	100. 0 (36)	100. 0 (119)	100. 0 (223)	100. 0 (287)

we do not know the occupations of 3 percent; 6 percent were in education, and 3 percent in journalism. This leaves a total of 2 percent, or six individuals, whose primary career was in any part of the entire remaining range of businesses and professions.

This does not imply that only these six individuals made money by business or professional activities. With the widespread corruption in the Kuomintang it goes without saying that a career in politics or the army was likely to be associated with extensive private business activity; but we may still distinguish between businessmen, few in number, who got into politics on the side, and the many politicians who seized upon the number of business opportunities which were made available by the very nature of a given political office. The picture may be clarified by looking at the main sources of income of the members of the first three CEC's. (Such data are not available for the other bodies in our sample.) The members of the CEC whose main income was from their party or government or army salary were outnumbered by more than two to one by those whose main source of income was nonpolitical (see Table 9). Yet as we have seen, their main career activity was political. Most of their time was spent on politics, but most of their income came from private enterprise. This apparent contradiction is explained when we realize that very few (6 out of 43) had a major source of private _earned_ income. Most of those with large

TABLE 9. SOURCES OF INCOME OF KUOMINTANG CEC MEMBERS, 1924–29

Salaries		
Government	2	
Party	8	
Military	4	
Total political		14
Land rents	12	
Interest on		
investments	11	
Business		
Large	—	
Medium	2	
Small	1	
Professional fees	2	
Wages	1	
Total private		29
Don't know		27
Total		70

private incomes lived on rent or interest. Their business dealings were not such as to conflict with the active pursuit of politics as a career.

Thus we see that the leadership of both Kuomintang and Communist Party were a young, Western-educated and Western-oriented group of professional politicians. (The term Western includes the U.S.S.R.) They were without roots in the normal enterprises of civilian life. Alienated and relatively hopeless of their futures in traditional careers, many found in revolutionary party politics new and appealing opportunities. Turning to the muddied waters of politics, they made their careers in the three main channels of political activity: organization, violence, and symbol manipulation.

In China the symbol specialists were relatively few as compared to their role in some other states. In the Hoover Institute Elite Studies we have found that the balance between these three kinds of political specialist is a highly significant index to the nature of the society. Among the stable cabinets in the West, for example, we found the role of army officers in Germany far greater than in Britain, France, or the United States, although even in Germany they were only about one-third as frequent as in either party in China. In the Politburo we found that in the course of time the specialists on organization and domestic violence supplanted the specialists on persuasion. In the Nazi elite we found that the specialists on organization dominated the specialists on persuasion. In the French Third Republic, however, the reverse was true: there the specialist on persuasion had the leading role.

In China, revolutionary chaos gave the specialist on violence (i.e., the military careerist) a larger role than anywhere else so far studied, and the role of the symbol specialists (lawyers, journalists, teachers) was considerably reduced. In both the Communist Party and the Kuomintang, persons with organizational and administrative careers constituted about half of the elite. Next most numerous were persons with military careers, who made up about one-third and increased in number with the passage of time. The residue is small, but it is interesting to note that among all the remaining professions education and journalism were the only ones sufficiently frequent to be of note. The nonpersuasive professions, e.g., engineering, were completely out. Lawyers, the dominant symbol specialists in stable Western elites, were here completely absent. But then lawyers have never played the same role in China as in the West. The few ideologizers included in the elite were those who could make a mass appeal.

The dominance of men of violence is an index of the intensity of revolutionary struggles. The young elite in China, seeing no stable future for themselves in the backward economy of their homeland, were expressing a self-confirming expectation. In their hopelessness of stable careers they turned to violent politics which, in fact, ultimately destroyed the chances for stable evolution. The career opportunities outside of politics gradually narrowed, and the standard of living gradually declined. This, plus the shattering of the old society, plus the slow spread of Western stimuli, and thus political activity, to ever wider circles of the population, gradually lowered the social status of the political elite.

It is easy to assume that the transfer of power from Kuomintang to Communists has been the key factor in the decline of upper-class and the rise of lower-class personnel in the elite. As already implied, this is not the whole story. A gradual decline in the status of elite members was taking place in both parties. The final triumph of the Communists symbolized (and perhaps was partly caused by, rather than caused) the rise of the plebeians.

A pair of related trends was in operation both in the Kuomintang and the Communist Party. In the first place, the circle from which the elite were being recruited was gradually widening to include broader sections of the population. In the second place, with the chaotic condition of the Chinese economy, the members of the elite were suffering downward social mobility more often than upward. They were less well off than their parents.

On these points our data on Kuomintang members cover only the members of the first three CEC's, but even in these early committees we can see these trends in operation. The widening of the circles from which elite members were recruited is brought out in Table 10. In it we find that (omitting the individuals on whom we do not have any information) the proportion of new members joining the CEC whose social status was lower-middle class or lower class went from 10.0 percent in 1924 to 17.6 percent in 1926 and to 31.3 percent in 1929. Thus, in the course of five years, the plebeians who succeeded in reaching the CEC rose from one in ten to one in three.

TABLE 10. SOCIAL STATUS OF NEW MEMBERS OF KUOMINTANG CEC

	1924		1926		1929	
	No.	Percent	No.	Percent	No.	Percent
Lower or lower middle class	2	10.0	3	17.6	5	31.3
Upper, upper middle, or middle middle class	18	90.0	14	82.4	11	68.7
Total known	20	100.0	17	100.0	16	100.0
Don't know	4		6		7	
Total	24		23		23	

On the whole these plebeians had plebeian fathers, and the men of higher social status had fathers of higher social status. However, the sons were having trouble maintaining their social status, or at least their income. More of them found that their incomes and statuses were declining rather than rising.

When we study an elite we normally expect and assume that we are dealing with a group which has experienced upward social mobility. Our sample is a preselected sample of successful men. The incompetent, the lazy, the ineffectual are excluded from it. Except where status is strictly hereditary, we may take it for granted that some of those in the top positions have risen from lower ranks, and so we may assume that, among the elite, upward social mobility is more common than downward mobility. In some sense this must have been true in China, too. The men in our sample had reached the top political positions, while few of their fathers had such exalted status. But in another sense the political elite was not rising. As they rose politically, they were losing out by other standards of status. Whereas, normally, political advancement means economic and social advancement also, in the shattered economy and society of modern China the reverse has been the case. The men who turned to politics were men who were otherwise on the skids. Their rise even to the top positions in politics did not altogether check their financial decline. Of the members of the first three CEC's of the Kuomintang 57 percent had the same general social status as their fathers (see Table 11). Of the remaining 43 percent only 18 percent had moved up while 25 percent had moved down.

TABLE 11. SOCIAL MOBILITY OF MEMBERS, 1924–29
KUOMINTANG CEC

Class Status of Son	Class Status of Father				
	Upper	Upper middle	Lower middle	Lower	
Upper	12	3	1	—	Moved
Upper middle	5	9	1	2	up, 8
Lower middle	1	4	4	1	(18%)
Lower	—	—	1	—	Stayed
	Moved down, 11 (25%)				put, 25 (57%)

The Chinese political elite was a socially declining and discomfited elite. That this was true of the Communists is not surprising. Communist leaders are often recruited from deprived strata of the middle class. In China, however, what was true of the Communists was true of both major parties. We may follow the trend for Politburo members from 1921 right through to 1945. When we do so the tendencies which we saw in operation in the Kuomintang CEC during the five years from 1924 to 1929 became much more apparent and may be seen to go further. In Table 12 we compare the men who joined the Politburo in 1929 and before with those who first joined after. Those whose fathers were peasants or proletarians rose from one-third to two-thirds of those on whom we have information. Specifically, what was taking place was a rise in peasant leadership. The rise of Mao to power, and the emergence of Soviet areas in the hinterland was accompanied by the replacement of intellectuals of middle-class and upper-class backgrounds by sons of peasants. This trend we wish to explore further, but before we do so let us note the role of the army in this change.

TABLE 12. OCCUPATIONS OF FATHERS OF POLITBUROCRATS

Father's Occupation	Date First Joined Politburo	
	1921–28	1931–45
Peasant	3	7
Proletarian	1	1
Scholar, scholar-official	4	1
Landlord	3	2
Merchant	1	1
Total known	12	12
Don't know	15	3
Total	27	15

The army played a central role in changing the social characteristics of the political elite. The complex picture may be summarized in the statement that the decline of the manipulators and the rise of men of violence was simultaneously the decline of the old high-status, educated, governing class and the rise of new social strata. Spelled out more fully the picture reveals the following facts:

1. The number of military men in the elite grew.
2. The economic status of soldiers rose.
3. The economic status of the members of scholar-official governing families severely declined.
4. The army brought less educated men into the elite.
5. The army elite, although largely upper class in origin, provided a channel by which even the son of a peasant could reach the top.
6. The army recruited in the more disorganized, less Westernized areas of China.

While we note each of these facts separately, let us keep in mind the central point which all of them illustrate: that the rise of the soldier broadened and democratized the recruitment of the Chinese elite. At the same time it helped undermine the traditional fabric of Chinese society and the potential for humane and stable development. These central facts may be seen in the development of both the Kuomintang and the Communist Party into military movements.

1. The increase in the number of soldiers in the Kuomintang CEC may be seen in Table 8 above. Ever since 1929 the proportion of military men in the CEC has remained above one-third. Undoubtedly the 1929 peak in the percentage of Committeemen with primarily military backgrounds was closely related to the growing power of Chiang Kai-shek. In the earliest committees personal relations with Dr. Sun Yat-sen had been important. Thereafter, the characteristics of various committees seem to have been closely related to factors in the career of Chiang Kai-shek. By 1929 Chiang's military position was strong, but his apparatus for political control (both in Party and Government) had not yet been perfected. Military men, there-fore, dominated the 1929 committee, and they continued to be a major force thereafter.

In similar fashion in the Communist Party the rise of military men may be tied to the rise of Mao and his policy of peasant revolt and guerrilla bases. In both parties the intellectuals (such as Sun Fo and Ch'en Tu-hsiu) came first, and the soldiers (such as Chiang and Chu Te) came later.

2. Through the army and the opportunities for economic exploitation which it yielded, many of the Kuomintang military elite succeeded in be-coming wealthy. The troubled waters of China's economy may have been a bleak prospect for the ambitious young technician, but they yielded good fishing for the soldier. Needless to say, this source of income was not usually his military salary. Only four of seventeen soldiers on the CEC (about whom we have information) relied primarily on their military sala-ries. Two more depended on Party salaries, while six lived mostly on rent and three more mostly on investments.

From these extracurricular activities they managed to obtain a higher income than their colleagues in the elite who were not soldiers (see Table 13). This was not because their fathers were richer. The wealth of their fathers was almost on a par with that of the rest of the elite. They became

TABLE 13. FINANCIAL STATUS OF SOLDIERS AND OTHER MEMBERS
OF KUOMINTANG CEC, 1924–29

Financial Status	Soldiers	Others
Upper	7	8
Upper middle	8	11
	15	19
Middle	1	3
Lower middle	2	8
Lower	—	4
	3	15
Total known	18	34
Don't know	5	13
Total	23	47

more prosperous than their nonmilitary colleagues who were suffering an economic decline. Only the soldiers did not suffer this decline.

3. We noted above the surprising fact that the Kuomintang CEC members were on the whole poorer than their fathers. Since this is not true for the military, it is even more strikingly true for Party organizers — the other major segment of the elite. Table 14 suggests what was happening to the established elite strata of China, from among which the organizers were recruited. They were caught in a squeeze from which even the most successful were seldom able to escape.

TABLE 14. MOBILITY OF SOLDIERS AND OTHER KUOMINTANG ELITE MEMBERS

Son's Financial Status Compared with Father's	Soldiers	Other CEC Members
Higher	5	3
Same	10	15
Lower	2	9

4. This squeeze, as we have said, affected the educated scholarly groups from which China had long drawn her political leadership. The soldiers were educated, in that they had attended military schools and sometimes other schools too, but they did not have the liberal education of their colleagues. Sixty-five percent of the soldiers on the Kuomintang CEC had studied only in China as compared with 30 percent of the nonsoldiers. Furthermore, the soldiers did not come from the scholar-official families which had provided much of China's political leadership in the past. These carriers of Chinese culture scorned the military life. Ten Kuomintang CEC members had scholar fathers. Of these only one was a soldier. Similarly, in the Communist Party a number of the early intellectuals in the Party came from families in the scholar-official tradition, but the later military leaders came from other—often peasant—backgrounds.

5. The peasants did not scorn the army. For them entry in the army represented not a comedown but a rise in social status.

Fei Hsiao-tung, on the basis of his experience in the study of communities in many different parts of China, remarked:

"In a village where farms are small and wealth is accumulated slowly, there are very few chances for a landless man to become a landowner or for a petty owner to become a large landowner. It takes generations to climb the ladder of success simply by frugality; and during these long years the prospect of periodic upsets, from natural sources such as famine or from personal misfortunes such as illness and death must always be faced. . . . It is not going too far to say that in agriculture there is no way really to get ahead."

A major function of military roles in Chinese culture is the provision of alternative possibilities to individuals of ambition who desire to improve their social, political, and economic fortunes but who realize that humble tilling of the soil, thrift, and virtue do not often bring success. [103]

As we shall note below, the Chinese Communist army certainly provided a channel of social mobility for the peasants. To some extent the Kuomintang army did too; all three members of the first three CEC's who came from peasant backgrounds were soldiers.

6. We have no later figures on fathers' occupations for the CEC, but all through, from 1924 to 1945, we find that the origin of the soldiers was the hinterland. This was also, we might add, the area of famine and disorganization in which the Communists recruited.

The coastal areas, where big cities, trade, commerce, and Western influence were dominant, led in providing the organizers for the Kuomintang. In particular this was true of the three provinces, Kwangtung, Chekiang, and Kiangsu. Canton is in Kwangtung (with Hong Kong near by): Shanghai is in Kiangsu with Chekiang close by. Even though Chekiang was the home of Chiang Kai-shek and a center of his machine, organizers rather than soldiers came from there, as they did from Kwangtung and Kiangsu too.

On the other hand, the Yangtze basin and the southern interior provinces of Yünnan and Kwangsi provided the soldiers.

The same ecological division between military leaders and others prevailed in the Communist leadership. As we shall see more fully below, the early intellectual leaders of the Party tended to come from around Shanghai, but the soldiers who led the Party in its later phase as a military movement tended to come from the Yangtze basin.

The ecology of the elite was thus more than a geographic matter. The geographic origins of the organizers and soldiers index their political character as cosmopolitans, on the one hand, or men of more limited backgrounds, on the other. The essential point to be noted is that in both parties civil war promoted the political soldier, and thereby a plebeianization of the elite. The scholar-politicians with a humanistic heritage—despite political skills which often kept them in office as individuals—were crushed as a social stratum marked by respect and a continuing tradition.

A gradual disintegration of Chinese society was taking place. The imperial elite of scholar-officials who were sons of scholar-officials had given way by the early 1920s to a new elite of young, Western-educated, Western-oriented revolutionaries. Many of them were still sons of scholar-officials, although many were also sons of businessmen or landlords. But they themselves, although often educated for a business or professional career, became, above all, party politicians. Their incursion into revolutionary politics stemmed from frustration, the frustration of a disorganized colonial economy; but politics did nothing to check that frustration, and indeed made it worse.

TABLE 15. BIRTHPLACES OF KUOMINTANG CENTRAL
EXECUTIVE COMMITTEEMEN
(In Percents)

Province of Birth	Soldiers	Others	All CEC Members
Coastal provinces			
Kwangtung	14.6	15.2	15.0
Chekiang	10.7	14.1	12.9
Kiangsu	5.8	9.8	8.4
Total from main centers of Western influence	31.1	39.1	36.3
Fukien	2.9	2.7	2.8
Shantung	1.9	2.7	2.4
Hopeh	3.9	4.9	4.5
Total from coastal provinces	39.8	49.4	46.0
Yangtze Basin			
Hunan	9.7	8.2	8.7
Szechwan	9.7	3.8	5.9
Hupeh	5.8	3.3	4.2
Anhwei	6.8	1.6	3.5
Total from Yangtze Basin	32.0	16.9	22.3
South interior			
Yunnan	3.9	.5	1.7
Kwangsi	4.9	2.2	3.1
Total from south interior	8.8	2.7	4.8
Total from areas listed	80.6	69.0	73.1

As time went on, their personal lot became worse more often than it became better. At the same time, the movement they had started and the
widening impact of Western thought began to stir new strata of the population. Lower-middle-class and peasant elements began to make their way
into both Kuomintang and Communist Party leadership. This they did partly
through their role as men of violence. With the deterioration of social order
in China, the army became an increasingly important channel to leadership.
(It was an extraordinarily important channel throughout the period.) The
social composition of the highest ranks of the army excluded scholars and
admitted a few peasants, and so its growing role facilitated the destruction

of the old elite and the plebeianization of Chinese political leadership. In both parties the rootless but educated professional revolutionary became the dominant leadership type.

Differences

Despite the common revolutionary character of both elites, some differences existed between the men who came to lead the Kuomintang and the men who came to lead the Communist Party. There were also differences between the major factions in the Kuomintang: left, right and followers of Chiang. And as we have already noted, there were differences between the earlier and later phases of the quarter century we are studying.

The most striking difference between the Kuomintang and the Communist Party elites was in their urban versus rural orientations. Both parties, as we noted, recruited at first among upper-class and middle-class circles and later also among lower-middle-class circles. However, the characteristic Communist leader was the son of a landlord or rich peasant, whereas the characteristic Kuomintang leader was the son of a merchant or other urban person.

The Marxian prognosis of proletarian revolution has never been confirmed. The revolt against the businessman has indeed occurred, but it has found its greatest strength not in industrialized societies where proletarian masses were highly organized and strong, but in backward peasant economies. After the first World War backward Russia proved "the weakest link" of the capitalist chain. There a small coterie of petty bourgeois intellectuals led a revolution in a country where 80 percent of the population was peasant. Since then the pattern has been repeated in other parts of the world.

In China, likewise, we find a Communist leadership which started out as a combination of rural rebels and urban professionals overthrowing a party whose leadership was distinctly business class. In the Communist Party leadership, there were few proletarians and also few sons of merchants. At first there was a goodly sprinkling of men from professional or intellectual families — men who gave the initial ideological impetus. Along with these, and increasingly dominant, however, were a group consisting of sons of peasants or sons of landlords. In this sense the Chinese Communist movement was indeed an agrarian revolution. It may have picked up and captured, or been captured by, the ideology of proletarian communism as interpreted in Moscow, but its social dynamic may be seen in the dominance of rural characters and urban intellectuals in the Communist Party; whereas business-class persons dominated the Kuomintang.

As we see in Table 16, merchants' sons were almost half of the identifiable members of the Kuomintang CEC's through 1929. (We lack later data on the Kuomintang.) In the same period they constituted 8 percent of the Politburo members and remained at this low level later (cf. Table 11). Even if we add the proletarians to the businessmen, the entire group of those

TABLE 16. RURAL-URBAN DISTRIBUTION OF ELITES
AS ESTIMATED BY FATHER'S OCCUPATION

	Kuomintang CEC 1924–29		Politburos		Communist CC 1945	
	No.	Percent	No.	Percent	No.	Percent
Landlords	14		5		8	
Peasants	3		10		11	
Total rural	17	38	15	65	19	73
Scholars, of-ficials*	6		4		3	
Merchants	22		2		2	
Proletarians	—		2		2	
Total urban	28	62	8	35	7	27
Total known	45	100	23	100	26	100
Don't know	25		19		18	
Total	70		42		44	

*Not elsewhere included.

stemming from the capitalist economy was only one-sixth of the Communist leaders.

Another group which can be classified as probably urban includes sons of fathers in professions, intellectual pursuits, or other nonbusiness type middle-class activities. One-third of the early Politburos consisted of such members of the intelligentsia (cf. Table 12). At that same period men of this character were but one-sixth of the Kuomintang CEC. They were thus far more prominent in the Communist movement, but they did not stay so long. Just as in the Soviet Politburo, men of rural origins replaced these intellectuals, who had given the movement much of its original stimulus.

Even from the beginning, however, half of the Communist leadership, as contrasted to only one-third of that of the Kuomintang, was rural in origin. With the triumph of Mao and his peasant orientation, that half rose to three-quarters.

TABLE 17. RURAL-URBAN DISTRIBUTION OF POLITBURO

	1921–28	1931–45
Rural	6	9
Urban	5	3
Total known	11	12
Don't know	16	3
Total	27	15

We cannot trace trends in the Kuomintang as well as we have those in the Communist Party since our data run out after 1929. But if we look at the trends from 1924 through 1929 we find that, just as the Communist Party was growing more rural with time, the Kuomintang was becoming more urban and more of a business-class party. In the first three Kuomintang CEC's the members whose fathers were merchants went up from 31 percent to 47 to 64 percent of those on whom we have information (cf. Table 18). At the same time, although not quite so smoothly, the propor-

TABLE 18. RURAL-URBAN DISTRIBUTION: NEW MEMBERS
KUOMINTANG CEC, 1924–29

	1924	1926	1929
Landlords' sons	7	4	3
Peasants' sons	–	1	2
Total rural	7	5	5
Scholars', officials' sons*	4	2	–
Merchants' sons	5	8	9
Proletarians' sons	–	–	–
Total urban	9	10	9
Total known	16	15	14
Don't know	8	8	9
Total	24	23	23

*Not elsewhere included.

tion of those whose own main sources of income came from rents declined, and the proportion of those whose main income was earned effected a rise. If these trends continued after 1929, as they probably did, then the split between Kuomintang and Communists became increasingly a split between business-oriented and rural-oriented young professional revolutionists.

The same thing stands out if we look at the geographic origins of the elites. The Kuomintang elite came more extensively from the coastal areas, particularly around Shanghai and Hong Kong, while the greatest concentration of Communist leaders was from Central China—the basin of the Yangtze. This may be seen in Map 1 which indicates the Provinces from which the elite of each party was distinctly more or less numerous than the population of the province would lead one to expect.

The provinces immediately around the main international ports are Kwangtung, Kiangsu, and Chekiang. As noted above, Hong Kong and Canton, the original home of the Kuomintang Government, lie near and in Kwangtung; Shanghai in Kiangsu with Chekiang close by. In the 1926 census these three provinces reported 22 percent of the population of China. In contrast to that figure we find that 36 percent of the Kuomintang CEC members came

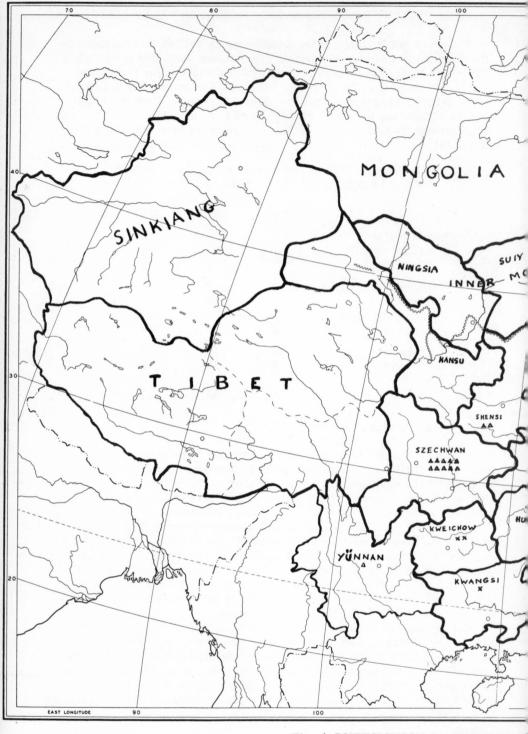

Fig. 1. DISTRIBUTION OF KUOMINTAN
COMPARED WITH THAT O

DIFFERENCE BETWEEN PERCENTAGE OF TOTAL POPULATION
AND PERCENTAGE OF C E C MEMBERS COMING
FROM EACH PROVINCE
Δ = UNDERREPRESENTATION BY 1/2 PERCENTAGE
POINT OR 2.25 MILLION PEOPLE
X = OVERREPRESENTATION BY 1/2 PERCENTAGE
POINT OR 2.25 MILLION PEOPLE

SCALE

| 0 | 100 | 200 | 300 | 400 | 500 MILES |

| 0 | 200 | 400 | 600 | KILOMETERS |

BONNE'S EQUAL-AREA PROJECTION

ENTRAL EXECUTIVE COMMITTEE
ENERAL POPULATION

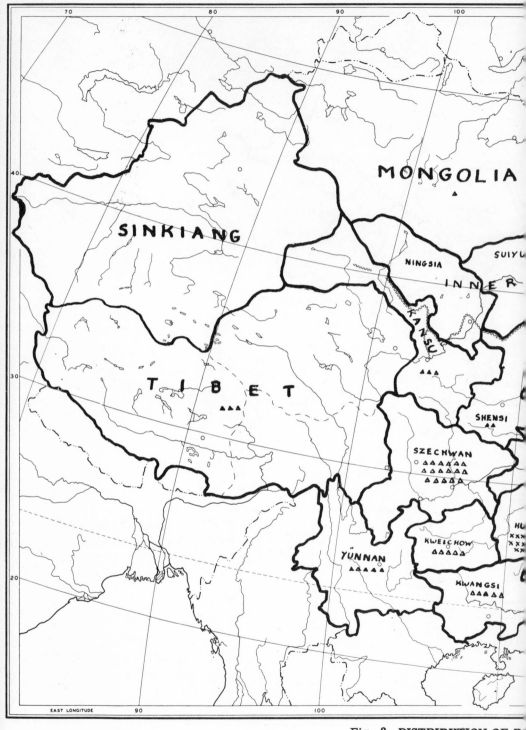

Fig. 2. DISTRIBUTION OF P…
WITH THAT OF G…

DIFFERENCE BETWEEN PERCENTAGE OF TOTAL POPULATION
AND PERCENTAGE OF POLITBURO MEMBERS COMING
FROM EACH PROVINCE
Δ = UNDERREPRESENTATION BY 1/2 PERCENTAGE
        POINT OR 2.25 MILLION PEOPLE
X = OVERREPRESENTATION BY 1/2 PERCENTAGE
        POINT OR 2.25 MILLION PEOPLE

SCALE

| 0 | 100 | 200 | 300 | 400 | 500 MILES |

| 0 | 200 | 400 | 600 | KILOMETERS |

BONNE'S EQUAL-AREA PROJECTION

BURO MEMBERS COMPARED
AL POPULATION

from those three provinces while only 19 percent of Politburo members
and 14 percent of the members of the 1945 Central Committee of the Com-

TABLE 19. ECOLOGICAL DISTRIBUTION OF PARTY ELITES

	Percent of China's Total Population of 1926*	Birthplaces		
		of CEC Members (Percent)	of Politburo Members (Percent)	of Communist C. C. 1945 (Percent)
South and Central Coast				
Kwangtung	7.6	15.0	4.8	2.3
Fukien	3.0	2.8	—	6.8
Chekiang	5.0	12.9	2.4	—
Kiangsu	7.1	8.4	11.9	11.4
Central interior				
Hunan	8.4	8.7	19.0	27.3
Szechwan	10.7	5.9	2.4	13.6
Hupeh	5.9	4.2	11.9	11.4
Anhwei	4.2	3.5	9.5	2.3
Kiangsi	5.7	5.2	2.4	4.6
South interior				
Kwangsi	2.5	3.1	—	2.3
Kweichow	2.3	3.5	—	2.3
Yunnan	2.3	1.7	—	
North				
Shantung	7.1	2.4	2.4	2.3
Hopeh	8.0	4.5	—	—
Honan	7.3	.4	—	—
Shansi	2.5	3.1	2.4	6.8
Shensi	3.6	2.8	2.4	2.3
Kansu	1.5	1.4	—	—
Tibet	1.3	1.1	—	—
Sinkiang	.5	.4	—	—
Mongolia	‡	1.4	—	—
Manchuria	9.9	2.8	—	4.5
Abroad	—	1.1	—	—
Don't know	—	3.8	28.6	—
Number		(287)	(42)	(44)

*Post office estimate. The China Yearbook, 1931, p. 2.
‡Not included in estimate. In other estimates Mongolia's population is a little over
2 percent of China's.

munist Party were born there. The Kuomintang drew its leaders from those
areas where Western and urban influence had penetrated most deeply, while
the Communists came rather from the rural hinterland.

To a somewhat lesser degree the same pattern may be seen if we add to
the three provinces immediately around Shanghai and Hong Kong the three

other coastal provinces of China proper: Fukien, Shantung, and Hopeh. Because these extend into the northern area, where both the Communists and Kuomintang were weak at first, not much of the leadership of either party came from them. Yet 40 percent of the 1926 population of China lived in the six coastal provinces together. From them came fully 46 percent of the Kuomintang leaders, but only 21 percent of the Politburo members and 23 percent of the members of the 1945 Communist Central Committee.

Besides being concentrated on the coast and around the major cities, the other notable geographic characteristic of Kuomintang leaders was that they were South Chinese. As the maps indicate, the heart of the old Chinese Empire in the north— Shantung, Honan, and Hopeh— gave few leaders to either of the new revolutionary elites. An examination of Chinese upheavals since 1850 reveals South China as a revolutionary incubator, while the north has been more conservative. To begin with, the southern regions, which were last conquered by the Manchus and which were furthest from the center of Manchu culture in Peking, were also the regions which had experienced longest contact with the West. Moreover, large numbers of southern Chinese had emigrated overseas where they came directly under foreign influences. It was from this group, indeed, that Sun Yat-sen won his first revolutionary support. There is some coincidence of revolution and areas of flood and famine, notably in the Yangtze Valley, where a preponderance of the Communist elite originated. Thus there may be more than symbolism in the fact that Kuomintang centers of origin looked outward, while many leaders of communism rose from areas of misery. Yet the region of "China's sorrow" along the Yellow River yielded few Communist leaders.

The geographic distribution of elite members shows not only the influence of certain general regional differences, but also the impact of party organization. Disproportionate numbers of leaders come from certain specific provinces where well-developed machines took hold and assumed national importance. Just as there is the Missouri factor in current American politics, so there was a Chekiang factor in Kuomintang politics. Chekiang was the home of Chiang Kai-shek, and as his clique of military men gained power, the number of native sons of Chekiang entering the Kuomintang CEC gradually rose from one in 1924— before Chiang became a CEC member— to nineteen in 1945 or the largest number from any one province. For similar reasons Kwangtung, the original home of the Kuomintang, was consistently overrepresented. Also the strong representation of Hunan and of Kiangsi on the Communist Party Politburos is in part the result of the development of strong Communist organizations (soviets) in those two areas.

Besides differences in geographic distribution and differences in rural-urban distribution, two other differences distinguish the Kuomintang and Communist leaderships. For one, the Politburocrats were somewhat younger than the Kuomintang CEC members. The former typically joined the Politburo at about age thirty or shortly thereafter, while the latter typically reached CEC membership in his early forties (cf. Table 6). Thus it took longer to reach recognition in the Kuomintang than in the Communist Party.

The elites of these parties also differed somewhat in their educational backgrounds. While it is not possible to make any flat generalization that one group was better or worse educated than the other, they did receive their educations in somewhat different places and types of institutions.

The Communist leadership contained a few more individuals with no formal higher education, though even among the Communists these were but a sprinkling. There were two such individuals on the Politburo (or 5 percent) and three such individuals on the 1945 Central Committee of the Communist Party (or 7 percent). In the Kuomintang CEC's there were only two such individuals (or one percent).

On the other hand, a larger proportion of the Communist leadership than the Kuomintang leadership had gone abroad for some of their higher education. The main reason for this is that much of the Communist leadership was Russian trained. Only 5 percent of the Kuomintang CEC members had studied in Russia while 48 percent of the Politburo members and 57 percent of the 1945 Communist Party Central Committee members had done so. (The Soviet Universities which have specialized in training the Communist Far Eastern leadership are indicated in Table 20.)

TABLE 20. SOVIET UNIVERSITIES ATTENDED BY COMMUNIST CC MEMBERS

University	Number
University of Moscow	1
Toilers of the Far East	7
Sun Yat Sen University	6
Red Army Academy	4
Lenin Institute	2
Don't know	7

While Communist training in Russia was the most common kind of foreign education, it is not that type of training alone which accounts for the extensive foreign study of the Communist leaders. As can be seen from Table 5, many of the Communists, as well as many of the Kuomintang leaders, studied in universities in capitalist countries—many of them, in fact, in countries of the West.

There was, however, an interesting difference in the countries in which they studied. Those who studied in France, especially those under the worker-student plan, tended to go left, whereas those who studied in the United States or Japan seemed to go right. From the very beginning those who had been students in France formed an important core of the revolutionary movement in the Far East. The first leader of the Chinese Communist Party, Ch'en Tu-hsiu, was one of the group of French-trained intellectuals who gave an important start to the development of communism in the Far East. It might be noted that among this group are not only leaders of the Chinese Communist Party, but also such other Far Eastern Communist leaders as Ho Chi Minh. Obviously, mere familiarity and contact with the West did not assure acceptance of Western ideas.

Modernization and democratization were too far from the realities of the Chinese situation to instill in the Chinese students who met them abroad a placid acceptance of the status quo. The contrast between the aspirations imported from the West and the possibilities actually open in the Chinese situation was so glaring as to turn all of them revolutionary. Certain social determinants such as family background and educational experiences did apparently influence the brand of revolution the young uprooted politician turned to, but the social differences are so much smaller than the similarities that we may suggest that the crucial difference separating the Communist leaders from the Kuomintang leaders was not a social one so much as a personal psychological one. The Kuomintang, being established in power, got the careerists; the Communists got the ideologists. Few of the Communists had any careers or sources of income outside the movement. For a long time theirs was distinctly the harder lot. The corruption in the Kuomintang ultimately became notorious and was, perhaps, a major force in driving millions of Chinese into the arms of the Communists. It would be misleading to view the conflict as one between social stability and revolution, and certainly false to view it as a struggle between democracy and authoritarianism. Both movements were expressions of a prevailing malaise and disorganization. Both movements were ruthless, but the Communists were more successful in tapping the energies of those who sought moral justification for their activities while the Kuomintang drew those with privatized attitudes.

We do not imply that in this respect the Kuomintang was a single undifferentiated whole. On the contrary many conflicting tendencies within the Kuomintang may be differentiated. Specifically our data enable us to compare three tendencies: the left, the right, and the military faction around Chiang. The way in which the members of the various cliques were grouped into these three tendencies is indicated in Table 21. The definition of these tendencies changes with time. In 1924 "left" meant quite a radical orientation. By 1945 "left" meant anything left of Chiang. The definition of a tendency is in terms of the politics of that day, but allowing for this fact only strengthens and reinforces the conclusions which follow.

The shifts in power and composition of these three tendencies reveal how the Kuomintang gradually lost its popular touch. For one thing the left wing gradually lost out in the jockeying for power, as may be seen in Table 22. In the 1924, 1926, and 1929 Central Executive Committees combined, the left-wingers were almost half the total membership—thirty-four leftists, to thirty-six rightists and pro-Chiang members. Of the leftists, perhaps six were Communists, but even omitting those the leftists clearly played a major role in the early committees. By 1945 the three wings of the Committee were fairly evenly divided, with the pro-Chiang members slightly more numerous than the others. By 1945 only a quarter of the left-wingers of

TABLE 21. GROUPING OF CLIQUES

Left

- (7) Kuomintang left
- (8) Sun Fo clique
- (11) Reorganization clique
- (16) The Middle Group
- (4) CP Rebels
- (28) European-American clique
- (106) Local cliques

Pro-Chiang

- (12) Party veterans—supporters of Chiang
- (33) Whampoa regeneration clique*
- (32) Direct affiliates*
- (9) Quasi-direct affiliates*
- (16) Officials (military)
- (2) Naval clique
- (14) Political science clique
- (10) Northeastern (Manchurian) Army clique
- (10) Overseas
- (9) Officials

Right

- (117) C. C. clique
- (10) Chu Chia-hua clique

*These military men were included under the Chiang group in spite of individual personal views (possibly more to the left) because at that time they supported Chiang as a group.

Except in a minority of individual cases the clique affiliation was used to determine political position.

the 1924, 1926, and 1929 committees were still on the committee, while 40 percent of the rightists and two-thirds of the Chiang supporters had retained their posts (cf. Table 23). Looking the other direction—that is from 1945 back—we find that the newer members were Chiang supporters or rightists, while the leftists were to some extent an "old guard." Thus 10 percent of the leftists had been on the 1926 committee, as against only 3 percent of the Chiang supporters and one percent of the rightists. These old-guard leftists who retained their posts while their influence was gradually fading included such prominent individuals as Mme. Sun Yat-sen, Ku Meng-yü, Kan Nai-kuang, and Sun Fo.

TABLE 22. POLITICAL COMPOSITION OF KUOMINTANG CEC'S

| | 1924–29 | | 1945 | |
	No.	Percent	No.	Percent
Left	34	48.6	71	31.9
Pro-Chiang	21	30.0	79	35.4
Right	15	21.4	73	32.7
Total	70	100.0	223	100.0

The tendency of the left to become an old guard may also be seen in Table 24, which compares the ages of the members of the different factions. In 1929 the mean age of the leftists and rightists was about the same, although the Chiang supporters were somewhat younger, partly because they were largely soldiers (who can achieve prominence in youth) and partly because they were the rising revolutionary faction, many of whose members were just

TABLE 23. CONTINUATION IN OFFICE OF MEMBERS OF
DIFFERENT TENDENCIES*

A. Percentage of 1924, 1926, 1929 CEC Members Who Held Office in Each CEC							
Tendency	Number of Individuals	Percent Holding Office in Each Committee					
		1924	1926	1929	1931	1935	1945
Left	34	32.4	85.3	29.4	14.7	35.3	26.5
Pro-Chiang	21	14.3	19.1	95.2	90.5	76.2	66.7
Right	15	66.7	20.0	40.0	40.0	60.0	40.0
B. Percentage of 1945 CEC Members Who Held Office in Each Earlier CEC							
Left	71	5.6	9.9	9.9	8.5	40.9	100.0
Pro-Chiang	79	2.5	2.5	11.4	13.9	44.3	100.0
Right	73	1.4	1.4	9.6	9.6	32.9	100.0

*The political positions of individuals was not always the same in every committee, and also the criteria of Left and Right changed over the years. All Western Hills members were later either Left (4) or pro-Chiang (2). Seven of the earlier pro-Chiang group were later CC clique; of the pro-Chiang Right Wing in 1945, only one earlier Left was later listed as farther right, i.e., pro-Chiang. No earlier pro-Chiang men were later Left. To minimize the effect of these changes of classification and to demonstrate the general shift to the right independent of them, the classification of individuals is kept constant in section A of the table, but not in section B.

joining the committee. But in 1929 no left-right difference in age existed. By 1945, sixteen years later, a remarkable change had taken place. The leftists were largely fairly old men. The younger men who were just joining the Committee were more often rightists. In sixteen years the average leftist had become seven years older than the average rightist.

TABLE 24. AVERAGE AGE OF KUOMINTANG FACTION MEMBERS

	Members of 1924, 1926, and 1929 CECS: Average Age in 1929	Members of 1945 CEC: Average Age in 1945
Left	46.2	54.1
Pro-Chiang	41.2	51.7
Right	46.8	48.5

At the same time, as the new blood was going into the right rather than the left, the Chiang faction had moved further to the right and the Communists and Communist sympathizers had been eliminated from the left. In other words, what was taking place between the Communist Party and the Kuomintang was a process of polarization. As so often happens when a new revolution approaches, the political and social lines grew sharper and sharper, and the middle disappeared. The individuals who strove to bridge the gap between the Kuomintang rightists at one end and the Communist leftists at the other declined in influence. Those in the center tended to move one way or the other, and—perhaps most important of all—the social characteristics of the Kuomintang and the Communist Party became more divergent.

We have already noted a growing tension between the rural and merchant groups as represented in the two parties. It remains to be noted that the struggle between left and right in the Kuomintang was a similar struggle in miniature, and that the decline of the left and the rise of the right was one of the factors which made of the Kuomintang increasingly a merchants' party and decreasingly a landlords' or rurally oriented one. Table 25 shows

TABLE 25. RURAL-URBAN DISTRIBUTION OF KUOMINTANG FACTIONS
(As Estimated from Father's Occupation; 1924, 1926, 1929 CEC's)

Origin	Left	Pro-Chiang	Right
Rural	12	3	2
Urban	10	11	7
Don't know	12	7	6
Total	34	21	15

that on the first three Kuomintang CEC's 35 percent of the leftists were rural, as against 14 percent of the Chiang supporters and 13 percent of the

TABLE 26. OCCUPATIONS OF FATHERS OF CEC MEMBERS IN DIFFERENT FACTIONS, 1924, 1926, 1929

	Left	Pro-Chiang	Right
Wealthy landlord, or scholar-landlord	6	2	2
Scholar-official	—	1	2
Scholar	2	—	1
Merchant-scholar or wealthy merchant	3	3	1
Other landlords	3	1	—
Other merchants	5	7	3
Professional revolutionary	1	—	1
Wealthy peasant	—	—	—
Other peasant	3	—	—
Don't know	11	7	5
Total	34	21	15

rightists. At the same time we see (in Table 27) that the rightists who, through the years, looked to Chiang for leadership, had a higher social status than either the leftists or Chiang's personal clique. Whereas one-

TABLE 27. SOCIAL STATUS, MEMBERS OF KUOMINTANG FACTIONS, 1924, 1926, 1929

Status	Left	Pro-Chiang	Right
Upper	12	9	7
Upper middle	8	3	4
Lower middle	4	3	1
Lower	1	1	—
Total known	25	16	12
Don't know	9	5	3
Total	34	21	15

quarter of the Chiang clique on whom we have information had lower or lower-middle-class parents, and whereas one-fifth of the leftists on whom we have information came from such modest backgrounds, this was true for only one rightist out of twelve. Thus the right wing lacked the small popular leaven which the other factions had. In the early Kuomintang, and presumably later too, the left was the faction that gave expression to China's agrarian problems and the right was the faction of urban vested interests. In the long run it was the right which came to lead the Party.

The Chiang clique showed an interesting in-between tendency. They were urban, but of lower status than the right, and of lower status, even, than the left. They were the faction of the newly politicized and disoriented urban middle class. They did not come from the professional strata which had provided the imperial elite. It was, therefore, altogether appropriate that the main channel of social mobility which this group used was the army, which in China was traditionally scorned. The difference between the relatively stable vested interests represented by the right wing and the revolutionary upstarts of the Chiang factions shows up in table after table. The financial status of the Chiang clique was often lower than that of rightists and even of the leftists (Table 28). One-quarter of them had lower or

TABLE 28. FINANCIAL STATUS, MEMBERS OF KUOMINTANG FACTIONS, 1924, 1926, 1929

Status	Left	Pro-Chiang	Right
Upper	7	5	3
Upper middle	9	6	4
Middle	1	—	3
Lower middle	6	2	2
Lower	1	3	—
Total known	24	16	12
Don't know	10	5	3
Total	34	21	15

lower-middle incomes as against one-eighth of the rightists. The fathers of the rightists were often scholars or scholar-officials, that is men with the highest prestige in old China. Only 10 percent of the Chiang supporters had such honorable fathers as against one-quarter of the rightists (cf. Table 29). The rightists, partly following in their fathers' footsteps, also became specialists in organization and administration. The Chiang clique were

TABLE 29. SCHOLARS' SONS IN KUOMINTANG FACTIONS, 1924, 1926, 1929

Father's Status	Left	Pro-Chiang	Right
Scholars	4	2	4
Others	19	12	6
Don't know	11	7	5
Total	34	21	15

military specialists. They entered a new profession for the Chinese elite; none of their fathers had followed it; they did not continue an established pattern of family prestige (cf. Table 30). Their departure from the established lines of prestige may be seen in their education, too. The number of CEC members with a Chinese classical education declined drastically for all factions between 1929 and 1945. But it was from among the Chiang supporters that persons with this traditional training for leadership disappeared first. The Chiang supporters started going to military schools instead of studying the Chinese classics (cf. Table 31). Thus in the Kuomintang the lines between the experts in pen and purse, on the one hand, and the experts in guns, on the other, grew over the years. The increasingly influential right wing became more and more exclusively a group of party organizers and administrators, while the Chiang faction continued to consist of the military (cf. Table 30).

These two groups lived in a fairly successful association; the organizers and the military men complemented each other without too much friction. This may be seen by comparing survival chances on the Executive Committee. On the whole the followers of Chiang were the ones who managed to stay on most successfully from committee to committee. It will be recalled that two-thirds of the Chiang clique who were on the first three committees were still on in 1945. Similarly, of the 1945 committee a larger proportion of the Chiang clique had been on the 1935, 1931, and 1929 committees than of either the rightists or leftists. But the rightists also managed to hold on to their posts fairly well. Their special qualification as administrator was of political value. Both organizers and military men averaged 1.7 incumbencies per individual. That is to say the typical individual, whether army officer or party organizer was on more than one, usually two, Central Executive Committees in the course of his career (cf. Table 32). Those whose main careers were nonpolitical served slightly less often, averaging 1.4 incumbencies per person. Thus the professionals had a somewhat better survival chance. It made no difference whether they played their part in the field of battle or in the field of Party organization.

Success did depend, however, on coming from a major political center. Those who came from the provinces around Canton and Shanghai (Kiangsu and Kwangtung) tended to do well. They averaged 1.8 and 2.0 incumbencies each, respectively. For continued power, it was necessary to be part of a machine. The army was one. The Party organizations in the two major centers were two others.

The type of education received also affected the individual's survival chance. The two individuals with no higher education served only once. Those with only a Chinese education had 1.6 incumbencies apiece. Those who studied in France or Russia were apt to be leftists and so they enjoyed only 1.4 and 1.1 terms apiece on the average. On the other hand, those who studied in Japanese universities (the main schooling ground of the rightists) did very well. Those who went to Japanese universities averaged two committee memberships apiece, while those who went to Japanese military

TABLE 30. CAREERS OF CENTRAL EXECUTIVE COMMITTEEMEN ACCORDING TO POLITICAL AFFILIATION

| | 1924, 1926, 1929 | | | | | | 1945 | | | | | |
| | Left | | Pro-Chiang | | Right | | Left | | Pro-Chiang | | Right | |
	No.	Percent	No.	Percent	No.	Percent	No.	Percent	No.	Percent	No.	Percent
Organization and administration	16	47.1	11	52.4	10	66.7	31	43.7	24	30.4	57	78.1
Military	11	32.4	10	47.6	2	13.3	26	36.6	51	64.6	6	8.2
Education	2	5.9	—		1	6.7	8	11.3	1	1.3	5	6.9
Journalism	1	2.9	—		1	6.7	2	2.8	1	1.3	4	5.5
Other	1	2.9	—		—		2	2.8	1	1.3	1	1.4
Don't know	3	8.8	—		1	6.7	2	2.8	1	1.3	—	
Total	34	100.0	21	100.0	15	100.0	71	100.0	79	100.0	73	100.0

TABLE 31. EDUCATION OF CENTRAL EXECUTIVE COMMITTEEMEN ACCORDING TO POLITICAL AFFILIATION

	1924, 1926, 1929						1945					
	Left		Pro-Chiang		Right		Left		Pro-Chiang		Right	
	No.	Percent	No.	Percent	No.	Percent	No.	Percent	No.	Percent	No.	Percent
Japanese university	7	20.6	4	19.1	5	33.3	10	14.1	6	7.6	14	19.2
Japanese military	5	14.7	6	28.6	2	13.3	2	2.8	16	20.3	–	
Chinese university	9	26.5	4	19.1	2	13.3	19	26.8	11	13.9	46	63.0
Chinese military	8	23.5	7	33.3	1	6.7	24	33.8	49	62.0	5	6.9
Chinese classical	6	17.7	1	4.8	3	20.0	5	7.0	1	1.3	2	2.7
United States	4	11.8	3	14.3	3	20.0	15	21.1	4	5.1	15	20.6
France	2	5.9	1	4.8	1	6.7	4	5.6	2	2.5	3	4.1
Germany	1	2.9	1	4.8	1	6.7	3	4.2	2	2.5	8	15.1
Great Britain	2	5.9	2	9.5	1	6.7	2	2.8	5	6.3	4	5.5
Belgium	–		–		1	6.7	1	1.4	–			
Soviet Union	2	5.9	–		–		2	2.8	8*	10.1	1*	1.4
Other							1	1.4	–		2	2.7
None							–		1	1.3	–	
Don't know	6	17.7	–		3	20.0	5	7.0	1	1.3	3	4.1
Total	34		21		15		71		79		73	
Total military	9	26.5	9	42.9	2	13.3	25	35.2	57	72.2	5	6.9
China only	10	29.4	5	23.8	2	13.3	33	46.5	40	50.6	33	45.2

*All these men except for two under Chiang had military education. The two under Left were nonmilitary.

schools (which were also extensively attended by Chiang followers) average
2.2 incumbencies each. The most successful individuals of all, however,
were those with a Chinese classical education. They averaged 2.7 incumbencies apiece. Men with this kind of education became rarer and rarer
in the Chinese elite, but apparently these few had been well trained for

TABLE 32. AVERAGE NUMBER OF INCUMBENCIES PER INDIVIDUAL
FOR VARIOUS CATEGORIES OF KUOMINTANG CEC MEMBERS

Category	Number of Incumbencies	Number of Men	Incumbencies per Man
Total sample	474	287	1.65
By career:			
Organizers	243	145	1.68
Military	176	103	1.71
Other	45	32	1.41
Don't know	10	9	1.11
By education:			
Japanese university	83	42	1.98
Japanese military	58	26	2.23
Chinese university	136	86	1.58
Chinese military	152	88	1.73
Chinese classical	41	15	2.73
Chinese only	193	123	1.57
By place of birth:			
Kwangtung	84	43	1.95
Kiangsu	44	24	1.83

political struggle. They came from families with a political tradition and
were brought up to play at the game of statecraft, which they did with skill.

If there is any doubt as to the value of the political training received by
those who were brought up in families from the traditional political classes
of China, it is set at rest by the surprising discovery that these same
strata were not only the most successful in retaining power in the Kuomintang CEC, but also the most successful in retaining power in the Communist
Party Politburo. Of forty-two members of the Politburo six served four or
more times, seven served three times, and the rest served once or twice.
What sort of individuals were these six and seven men who managed to hold
office over various twists and turns of the party line. Of the six who served
four or more times, three were sons of scholar-officials. These three were
all but one of the scholar-officials' sons who ever reached the Politburo.
In other words, almost all these men were successful place holders, and

they were also half of all the most successful place holders. The other
half — that is, the other three individuals who served on four or more committees — included one son of a wealthy landlord, and two sons of wealthy
peasants. Thus the Politburo members with the best chance of survival
were generally upper class and correspondingly well educated. Specifically,
they came from families with a tradition of governing.

When we turn to the seven individuals who served on three Politburos,
we find a surprising paradox. They came from the lowest rungs of the
Politburo social ladder. Five of them were sons of peasants and of those,
three were not wealthy peasants. In fact those three were three out of the
four Politburocrats who were sons of poor or middle peasants. Similarly,
one of the two proletarians on the Politburo belonged to this group who
served three times. Thus four of the seven men in this group were of lower-
class origins.

What is the explanation of the strange phenomenon that the most successful Politburocrats were men of high-class origin and the next most successful men were of low-class origin, whereas the second rung in the Politburo
was filled by men in between? The answer arises from the two phases of
Communist development and the two groups of men — radical intellectuals
and discontented agrarians — who came together to create the Chinese Communist movement. The first group were the radical intellectuals, sons of

TABLE 33. PERSISTENCE ON POLITBURO BY FATHER'S OCCUPATION

Father's Occupation	Number of Times on Politburo		
	4 or More	3	1 or 2
Scholar-official	3		1
Wealthy landlord	1		2
Other landlord			2
Scholar-revolutionist			1
Merchant			2
Wealthy peasant	2	2	2
Other peasant		3	1
Proletarian		1	1
Don't know	—	1	17
Total	6	7	29

politicians themselves, most of whom (four out of six) came from Kiangsu,
that is, Shanghai or its vicinity. A little later they were joined by college-
trained young men from the land. These were, for the most part, the sons
of wealthy peasants or landlords, but those few who had the hardness and
determination to rise to the very top and stay there were the poorest of the
agrarian group. The sons of landlords and wealthy peasants filled the ranks

of those who served on only one or two Politburos, and many of them ultimately broke from the Communist movement. Out of twelve Politburocrats,
whose father's occupation we know, and who served on one or two committees, four were landlords and two were wealthy peasants, making together
one-half. Thus it was clear that the top leadership of the Communist Party
consisted of a team of scholar-politicians in the habit of ruling and were
the more hard-bitten of the peasant leaders.

The former group, the members of scholar-official families, were
successful in the Kuomintang. The latter group, sons of tillers of the soil,
did not rise in the Kuomintang, and that was its fatal weakness.

The picture which emerges from this statistical analysis of the leadership of the two leading Chinese parties of the past quarter century has been
summarized above in the one word, polarization. Both parties, as we have
repeatedly noticed, broke away from the traditional Chinese values and
forms of social organization. They were both revolutionary movements of
rootless professional politicians feeding on disorganization and chaos. The
Kuomintang, however, permitted itself to come increasingly under the control of backward-looking elements oriented toward securing personal economic advantage in business activities. Those factions and individuals
with other orientations were gradually squeezed out. At the same time the
Communist Party managed to transform itself from an intellectually oriented organization into a rural mass-oriented one. It made use of the ideological weapons which its early urban intellectual elements brought to it,
but it also managed to give some kind of expression to the strivings of
many young, Western-educated, discontented Chinese who were still sensi-
tized to the problems of their home environment, the rural village. These
problems were shared by most Chinese. In view of this polarization in the
composition and orientation of the two major parties in China, and in view
of the disorganization of Chinese society, it is not surprising that the struggle between parties eventually became civil war, nor is it surprising that
the Communists won.

V. DEVELOPMENTS UNDER THE PEOPLE'S GOVERNMENT

By the end of the Japanese War in August 1945, the relationship between the Kuomintang and Chinese Communist parties was such that civil war between them was almost inevitable. It was true that, during the first twelve months after the formation of the Kuomintang-Communist entente in September 1937, a series of concrete steps had been taken to bring about its implementation, and it was during this period that Chiang Kai-shek began to emerge as a symbol of Chinese unity. But as early as the closing months of 1938 Kuomintang-Communist relations had begun to deteriorate. In August of that year the Hankow-Wuchang Defense Headquarters outlawed three Communist-sponsored mass organizations on the basis that the Communists planned to use them for purposes of strengthening their positions in Nationalist territory. During succeeding months a number of similar Communist units was suppressed.

Considerable friction developed from the expansion of Communist military forces into areas outside the zones which had been assigned to them. This reached a climax in the New Fourth Army incident of January 1941, when Kuomintang forces attacked a Communist unit on the basis that the latter, wishing to expand its influence southward, had ignored a Nationalist order to engage the Japanese in the Yellow River area.

This and similar clashes led to periods of negotiation — with minor parties attempting to mediate — and to an American offer of good offices in 1944 by Major General Patrick J. Hurley, the personal representative of President Roosevelt. Despite long and tortuous negotiations, the two parties failed to reach a permanent understanding. It is true that Hurley reported an apparent readiness on the part of the Kuomintang and the Communists to co-operate. Moreover, Stalin personally assured him that the Soviet Union did not intend to recognize any government in China except that of the Nationalists with Chiang Kai-shek as its leader. But Chiang and Mao seemed more intent on furthering the interests of their respective parties than in co-operating, even in the face of Japanese aggression.

The United States, by force of circumstances had been assuming increasingly heavy responsibility for prosecuting the war against Japan. Now it was clear that amphibious drives across the Central and South Pacific had taken a shocking toll in American lives, and estimates of the probable human cost of assaults on Japan were causing considerable apprehension. By the early months of 1945 both soldiers and civilians demanded to know why the Soviet Union had not accepted a share of the fighting in Asia.

It was through these circumstances and out of Allied relationships with the Soviet Union that the Yalta Agreement emerged. In signing this document the United States and Great Britain paid a high price for Russian aid in a war which — although few outside Japan knew it — was all but won. The two Western powers, without consulting China, recognized a Soviet Russian claim to nearly all imperialist concessions on Chinese soil which Czarist Russia had lost to Japan through the Treaty of Portsmouth in 1905.

Essential aspects of this agreement served as a blueprint for the Sino-Soviet Treaty of Friendship and Alliance, August 14, 1945; however, the Soviet Union agreed in the latter document to give the National Government of China both moral and material support and offered formal assurances that the Soviet Union would not interfere in China's affairs. Largely because of this guaranty, the Sino-Soviet Treaty was well received at first in China and in the United States. Many observers concluded that the Soviet Union was ignoring the Chinese Communists, and there were speculations that both Russian and Chinese Communists had reconciled themselves to Chiang Kai-shek and the Nationalist Government. In retrospect it is clear that these observers did not understand the fundamental Communist tactic of co-operation combined with opposition. Within a few months Nationalist and Chinese Communist troops were engaged in a full-scale civil war.

Military, political, and economic conditions resulting from the abrupt capitulation of the Japanese, the advance of Soviet troops into Manchuria, the appearance of vacuums resulting from the surrender of Japanese forces in China, and the Russians' stripping of Manchurian industry—all these developments aggravated a situation that was already potentially dangerous.

After the Japanese surrender, Communist troops began racing Nationalist armies for control of areas occupied by the Japanese. The Nationalist Government was estimated to hold a five-to-one advantage in troops and rifles and a near monopoly of transport, heavy equipment, and air strength. The Communists enjoyed a geographical advantage in being closer to many of the Japanese areas, including Manchuria.

The United States sought to help the Nationalists in their reoccupation of Japanese-held territory by transporting Nationalist armies by air to East and North China and more than 400,000 troops by water. United States Marines were detailed to hold key railroads and coal mines for the Nationalists. With this and other American assistance, Chiang Kai-shek's forces were able to accept the surrender of a great majority of the 1,200,000 Japanese troops in China proper. In Manchuria, however, the Nationalists did badly.

During the course of negotiations leading toward the Sino-Soviet Treaty, the Soviet Union had assured the Nationalists that Russian forces would evacuate Manchuria within three weeks after the Japanese surrender and that the withdrawal would be completed within a three-month period. When Russian troops began pulling out, however, the Nationalists, with extended lines of communication and limited transportation facilities, were unable to take over evacuated areas ahead of the Chinese Communists. The Nationalist Government found itself in the difficult position of having to ask the Russians to delay their departure.

When Soviet troops did evacuate Manchuria, they stripped the area of Japanese-built industrial equipment, but left behind for Chinese Communist forces valuable caches of Japanese rifles and a well-trained Communist army of local Chinese and former Japanese puppet troops. The Nationalists, risking the overextension of their lines, tried to reoccupy Manchuria through force of arms.

Incidents grew into open civil war, relieved, intermittently, by the uneasy truces which General Marshall's mission was able to achieve. President Truman had charged Marshall with the responsibility of bringing peace to China under conditions that would permit a stable government and progress along democratic lines and of assisting the Nationalist Government in establishing its authority over the widest possible areas of China. The first objective was not realizable. The greatest obstacle to peace, General Marshall reported, was the complete, overwhelming suspicion with which the Chinese Communist Party and the Kuomintang regarded one another. Marshall was bitterly critical of irreconcilable groups within the Kuomintang, interested only in preserving their own feudal control of China, and of "dyed-in-the-wool" Communists who used abuse, lies, and any other drastic measures, even to wrecking the economy of the country, in order to achieve their ends. The only solution, he said, lay in the assumption of leadership by liberals in the government and in the minority parties. These men and women, however, were few in number, without influence or support, and entirely unable to act.

The second objective of the Marshall mission—to help the Nationalists extend their authority—seemed easier to realize, since by early 1947 Chiang's government had reached a peak of military successes and territorial expansion. Chinese Communist generals, however, brought superior forces to bear at points of greatest Nationalist extension—just as they had done during Chiang's "bandit suppression campaigns" in the days of the Juichin Republic—destroying isolated bodies of troops, cutting communications, and seizing arms. Through these tactics they were soon able to supplement Russian-donated Japanese rifles with American weapons captured from American-trained and American-equipped Nationalist armies.

Chiang Kai-shek's troops rapidly lost their will to fight, and in October 1948 Nationalist defenders of Mukden defected to the Communists, taking with them valuable weapons and other equipment. Communist victories now followed one after the other: Tientsin fell on January 15, 1949; Peking surrendered without a fight; in April the Communists crossed the Yangtze; Shanghai fell in May, and on October 15 Canton, which had served as the Nationalist capital for the previous six months, capitulated without resistance. Chiang Kai-shek had already moved his headquarters to Formosa.

Strengths and Weaknesses

At this early point it is difficult to determine precisely which Kuomintang weaknesses and which Communists strengths, as well as what external factors, were critical in the overthrow of one elite and the coming to power of the other, but a number of factors are worth examining. It is clear that both leadership groups emerged from the political, social, and economic chaos accompanying the impact of Western culture upon Chinese

society and the breakdown of the Ch'ing Dynasty. Both began as relatively
unorganized intellectual movements instigated by scholars and professional
men, nearly all of whom had been educated abroad or had in one fashion
or another been influenced by Western culture. Many individuals in both
groups came from the same social and economic backgrounds—from landlord, scholar, or bureaucratic families, from merchant or moneylender
circles, or from the newly developed capitalist class of large cities along
the coast. These, of course, were the families who could afford to edu-
cate their sons in Japan or Europe and to provide them with incomes during long periods of exile or profitless political activity. Most leaders in
both groups rose to prominence through organizational and administrative
work within their respective parties, with a large majority attaining leadership through military service. Only a few built careers independent of
government or party, and most of these served in professional fields, such
as journalism and education, which were closely related to their Kuomintang or Communist activities. Both parties developed schisms and conducted purges, but neither tended to take drastic action against its own
dissidents. The Kuomintang was quite ready to kill Communists, however,
and vice versa.

The differences are equally noteworthy. The Kuomintang, which began
as a Western-oriented, middle-class revolutionary movement with undisciplined organization and ill-defined goals, became increasingly radical with
the introduction of Russian influence— but only up to the point where agrarian
revolution threatened the security of members springing from the landowning classes. At that contingency the Kuomintang leadership, seeking to
preserve both power and property, swung over into a course, increasingly
militaristic and counterrevolutionary, which servered their contact with,
and brought them into opposition to, a large section of the population, especially the peasant masses.

Once this turn had been made, it became clear that between so-called
radical and conservative wings of the Kuomintang the struggle for power
was more critical than disagreements over points of doctrine. Furthermore,
since neither wing was willing to carry out a program that would appeal to
peasant or labor masses, individual leaders found themselves compelled to
depend upon political manipulation, factional maneuvering, and the juxtaposition of military force.

As Chiang Kai-shek consolidated his personal power, Kuomintang cliques
became increasingly important as instruments of political expression. At
the same time Kuomintang leadership grew older, and although the Central
Executive Committee expanded more than nine times its original size,
support for Chiang became more and more a prerequisite for election to
that body.

The Communist Party, which began as a series of loosely organized intellectual discussion groups, accepted Russian Bolshevik organization and
discipline at an early date, whereupon leaders who hitherto had owed their
influence to literary or scholastic prestige came now to depend upon Moscow

for their mandate. The Party made no pretense to democracy in the Western sense; discipline was rigid; purges under Russian supervision at least as late as 1931 were conducted with every major shift in the tactical line. And when a policy failed, even though Stalin himself had made it, the most nearly responsible Chinese leader was commonly censured, whereupon he either recanted or suffered expulsion from the Party.

The outstanding exception, the only group who not only disagreed with Stalin but also succeeded in holding to its course, was that composed of Mao Tse-tung and his followers. They strapped a readjusted Russo-Marxist bridle over the peasant movement (the central force in the Chinese Revolution) and put themselves astride while Stalin and his associates were still trying to team them to another horse.

Kuomintang military men, except for Whampoa graduates, were likely to be officers trained in the old style of military leadership. Beyond this, many were independent or semi-independent war lords whose loyalty to the Kuomintang could not always be counted on. In contrast to these, the quality and dedication of Communist generals, whose military duties were often superimposed upon a host of Party responsibilities, may constitute one of the chief factors in the Communist Party success. Many of them had received in the Soviet Union specialized training in techniques of insurrection and perhaps also in twentieth-century mechanized warfare. Most had gained long experience as guerrilla leaders. Nearly all had submitted without qualification to Communist Party, as well as to military, discipline. Those who survived Chiang's "extermination campaigns," years of illegal underground activities, the vicissitudes of the Long March, and the battles of the Japanese War established long records of competence, loyalty, and dependability.

These various differences undoubtedly constitute some of the reasons for Communist successes and Kuomintang failures, but final evaluation must await a more thorough examination of the historical record than has yet been undertaken. To date it is almost impossible, for example, to determine the relationship, after the Long March, between the Chinese Communist Party and Stalinist leadership in Moscow. Chinese leaders, including Mao Tse-tung, have repeatedly acknowledged their acceptance of Bolshevik discipline and their sympathy with and loyalty to the Soviet Union. Recently Ch'en Po-ta, a Chinese Communist, in an effort to define the precise relationship between Mao and Stalin, stressed in glowing terms the Russian leader's insight and infallibility as a prophet of the Chinese revolution. Ch'en Po-ta wrote that because of language difficulties and "counterrevolutionary blockades," Chinese Communist leaders, including Mao, were not able to read the works of Stalin until comparatively recently. It happened, however, that Mao's ideas were "identical with those of Stalin, and consequently he was able to come to the same conclusions in regard to fundamental problems."[104]

But these are statements that cannot be accepted seriously. We know that from 1924 until 1932, at least, Moscow was in close touch with the

Chinese Communist leadership. Many individual Chinese studied in Moscow, and Stalinist agents were nearly always attached to Communist headquarters in China, but Mao Tse-tung's ideas were not identical with Stalin's. Whatever the effect of these rationalizations in China, to the non-Communist Western critic they suggest that the true relationship between Mao and Stalin has been sufficiently unorthodox in the past to require— at the moment of China's emergence as a major Communist power— a degree of public readjustment.

It may be recognized that the advance of Soviet Russian troops into Manchuria and the Russian policy of turning over captured Japanese arms to the Chinese Communists speeded this emergence. [105] But the comparative histories of Russian on-the-spot direction of the Chinese revolution from 1924 until 1931, and of Mao Tse-tung's long agrarian struggle suggest that it would be misleading, and from the American viewpoint dangerous, to underestimate the current strength of Chinese Communist leadership or to place it in the same general category with Communist elites in Eastern Europe, which have owed their existence almost entirely to the whims of Joseph Stalin.

The Backgrounds and Characteristics of Various Individual Leaders*

When we have analyzed group characteristics and general trends in leadership, there remains a whole series of questions about the capabilities and inclinations of various individual Chinese Communist leaders of the present day. Which men hold actual power, and are they secure in their positions? Are the top leaders on good terms with one another, or does competition for power produce dangerous personal frictions? What are the attitudes of these men toward their own country and toward the Soviet Union? Are they Communists first, or would they turn against the Soviet Union in case of a severe conflict between Russian and Chinese interests? None of these questions is easily answered.

It remains extremely difficult to establish reliable criteria for judging the personal inclinations and relative standing, prestige, and power of various Chinese Communist leaders. Unofficial and semiofficial listings of top party officeholders often differ in important detail, and equally competent observers are often in disagreement. Even the biographical details of important leaders are controversial and subject to constant correction. The result is that interpretations of internal Chinese Communist Party politics remain highly subjective and should be considered with caution.

---

*The following section includes material drawn from Robert C. North, "The Chinese Communist Elite," in H. Arthur Steiner (Ed.), "Report in China," The Annals of the American Academy of Political and Social Science, Vol. 227 (September 1951), pp. 70–74. Permission to reprint it here is gratefully acknowledged. A number of additions and corrections have been made on the basis of new data recently received.

Central Committee members are believed to be listed in order according to the number of votes received in the elections, and in this connection it is worth noting that membership in the Politburo does not seem necessarily to coincide with a high position on the Central Committee. As the roll is believed to stand at this writing, the first four—Mao Tse-tung, Chu Te, Liu Shao-ch'i and Lin Tsu-han (in that order)—are Politburo members, but there is at least considerable skepticism about the reported Politburo membership of the fifth Committeeman, Lin Piao. Politburo member Chou En-lai, on the other hand, stands nineteenth on the 1951 Central Committee listing (twenty-second on some earlier lists).

Investigations into the personal lives of Chinese Communist leaders generally fail to throw much light upon the internal politics of the Communist Party. Among those often listed by non-Communist sources as belonging to the Politburo are three "returned students"—Chang Wen-t'ien, Ch'en Shao-yü, and Wang Chia-hsiang. During the Cheng Feng or "ideological remolding movement" of 1942, Mao struck out fiercely at the "dogmatists" or "half-intellectuals" who had grounded themselves in Marxist-Leninist theory, but who remained incapable of wedding theory with practice. It is perhaps not certain that this attack was directed primarily against the "returned students," but it is true that these men dropped into temporary obscurity about that time. More recently the three have regained some prominence. Wang Chia-hsiang became the first new Chinese ambassador to Moscow late in 1949, returning from that post early in 1951 to become Vice-Minister of Foreign Affairs in the Central People's Government. Chang Wen-t'ien, in January 1950, was designated as the Central People's Republic permanent representative on the United Nations Security Council (still pending accreditation); in April 1951 he became ambassador to Moscow. Wang Ming, (Ch'en Shao-yü) has, from the beginning of the new regime, been chairman of the Law Commission of the Central People's Government. All three are members of the Central Committee of the Party, but it is now seriously doubted that they belong currently to the Politburo.

In addition to the three "returned students" noted above, non-Communist sources often list Lin Piao, P'eng Te-hua huai, and K'ang Sheng as Politburo members, although there has been no confirmation of their current membership.

Widely recognized for his ability as a military strategist and technician, Lin Piao is reputed to inspire his officers and men with exceptional loyalty and elan. In 1949, for example, when his Fourth Field Army was moving into Central China, Western observers reported that his troops tended to identify themselves, not by unit or simply as Communists, but as "Lin Piao's boys." After years of active military service and a sojourn (1937–42) in the Soviet Union, he led Chinese Communist troops into Manchuria in 1945, and was subsequently appointed commander of the Northeastern Democratic Army which captured Tientsin in January 1949. Some months later his troops, redesignated as the Fourth Field Army, proceeded into Central China and captured Hankow. In late 1950 he led the same army into Korea.

P'eng Te-huai, who is also sometimes listed by non-Communist sources as a Politburo member, stands second in the Chinese Communist military hierarchy. It was he who was in command of troops that captured, and soon lost, Changsha in 1930, and later his First Red Army Corps figured prominently in the Long March. There are indications that in recent years he has taken over important duties from his chief, the veteran Chu Te. Communist sources do not currently confirm his Politburo membership.

A subject of considerable speculation is K'ang Sheng, who may possibly have achieved notable, but largely unmeasured, power as chief of the Chinese Communist secret police. In the thirties he spent six years in Moscow, where he became closely associated with Wang Ming. Reportedly raised to the Politburo in 1943, he became chief of the Social Affairs Department of the Party Central Committee. In 1949 he assumed the post of Secretary to the Shantung Branch of the Party's East China Bureau, a post which, on the face of it, seems oddly anticlimactical. During months prior to this writing, moreover, K'ang Sheng has not appeared publicly, being absent even from important government meetings, and there have been unconfirmed reports to the effect that his presence has not been noted either in Peking or Shantung. There are strong reasons for doubting that he serves currently on the Politburo.

At this writing, the most reliable analysis of the Central Organization of the Communist Party of China is Current Background, No. 137, issued by the American Consulate General, Hong Kong, November 15, 1951. This document lists Kao Kang and Tung Pi-wu as "probably" belonging to the Politburo. Kao Kang's background is exceptional in that he rose to prominence in a relatively independent fashion. Born of a poor peasant family, he received no formal education, but joined the Communist Party in 1926, and took part in a series of guerrilla uprisings that pushed him into a position of leadership in Shensi, a region then quite apart from the chief area of Communist development. When the main columns of Communist armies terminated the Long March in Shensi, Kao was one of two outstanding figures in a soviet that had already been established there. Upon its dissolution he was elected an official in the Shensi-Kansu-Ningsia Border Region. At the close of World War II he was transferred to Manchuria, where he became head of the Northeast People's Government in August 1949. By some observers he is regarded as a figurehead who attained high office through his loyalty to Mao, while others consider him a strong man placed in the northeast by Mao in order to keep that area securely under Chinese control. Again, there is no decisive evidence, although his activities and prominence in northeastern developments suggest the latter view.

Tung Pi-wu, a founder of the Chinese Communist Party, became known to Americans as a member of the Chinese delegation to the United Nations Conference on International Organization in 1945. Like Lin Tsu-han, he was active in Sun Yat-sen's revolutionary movement long before the formation of the Communist Party. After the Communist-Kuomintang split, he fled first to Japan and then to Moscow, where he studied until 1931. After completing the Long March, he became president of the Central Party School, a position he had held previously during the existence of the Kiangsi Soviet. At the present time he is one of the four Vice-Premiers of the State Administrative Council in the Central People's Government.

Current Background, No. 137, makes the following tentative listing of men who almost certainly serve on the current Politburo: Lin Tsu-han; P'eng Chen; Ch'en Yün; Chu Te; Chou En-lai; Liu Shao-ch'i, deputy chairman; and Mao Tse-tung, chairman.

Lin Tsu-han, like Tung Pi-wu, is a veteran revolutionist and former close associate of Sun Yat-sen. After the Communist-Kuomintang split in 1927, he studied in the Soviet Union and in other European countries and founded a Chinese worker's school in Khabarovsk. A participant in the Long March, he later served as Commissioner of Finance in the Shensi-Kansu-Ningsia Soviet and became chairman in 1937, when it was transformed into the Border Region Government. At the present time he is serving as Secretary General of the Central People's Government.

P'eng Chen, after serving for three years as chairman of the Northeast Bureau of the Chinese Communist Party and political commissar to Lin Piao's United Democratic Army, became Secretary of the Peking Municipal Committee of the Party in February 1949. A member of the Communist Party since 1926, P'eng devoted many of his early years to the organization of trade-union activities in North China.

A leading Communist economist and labor expert, Ch'en Yün was appointed chairman of the Mukden Military Central Commission and chairman of the All-China Federation of Labor. With a primary school education, he worked for the Commercial Press and later for the Chung Hua Book Company in Shanghai. After joining the Communist Party in 1924, he participated in the Shanghai strikes of 1925 and 1927 and subsequently served as a labor union organizer under the Kiangsi Soviet. Between 1939 and about 1934 he served first as deputy chief and later as chief of the Department of Organization of the Communist Party. In 1949 he was reported as attending the Tenth All Union Congress of Trade Unions in Moscow.

Chu Te, commander in chief of the Chinese People's Liberation Army, was born in Szechwan in 1886, the son of a peasant father. After studying at the Yünnan Military Academy, he continued his education in Europe where, with Chou En-lai, he founded a Berlin branch of the Chinese Communist Party. After being deported from Germany, he returned to China by way of Moscow and was one of the leaders of the Nanchang Uprising in 1927. There was a time in the late thirties when the Chu-Mao combination was mistaken for one person by many Chinese, but despite Chu's twenty years as commander in chief of Chinese Communist armies, his political importance is believed to have remained secondary.

Among all Chinese Communist leaders, Chou En-lai is perhaps the most controversial. At one time or another, he has been described as "moderate," "Western-oriented," "orthodox," and "double-faced." While serving as negotiator at the time of Chiang Kai-shek's kidnaping at Sian in 1936, and later in Nanking, Chungking, and Peiping, he impressed many Westerners with his courtesy and apparent good will and "liberality." There are competent observers, on the other hand, who consider him powerful and crafty and who believe that his connections with Moscow are exceptionally close.

Born in 1898, of landlord antecedents, Chou En-lai has a notably cosmopolitan background. After attending middle school in China, he took training in Japan and then went to France under the worker-student plan. Together with Li Li-san and other Chinese students in Paris, he founded a French branch of the Chinese Communist Party in 1921, and later, while studying in Germany, joined with Chu Te in establishing a Berlin cell. After his return to China in 1924, he was appointed political instructor and acting chief of the Political Department of Whampoa Military Academy, where Lin Piao was one of his students.

Arrested during the Communist-Kuomintang schism, Chou En-lai escaped and subsequently went to Moscow for study. In September 1930 Chou was co-author of the "Report of the Third Plenum" which rebuked Li Li-san for overestimating the tempo of the Chinese revolution and for committing tactical mistakes, but which stated that the general line of urban insurrection was still "in complete harmony with the Comintern." During Li Li-san's subsequent trial before the Oriental Bureau of the Comintern, Russian Communist leaders condemned the other author, Ch'ü Ch'iu-pai, for his actions at the Third Plenum, but there is no evidence at hand that Chou En-lai was severely censured.

During the period of "returned student" leadership, Chou, according to one observer, was in charge of military affairs, superior to Chu Te, who was considered only a field commander. This same source states that Chou En-lai and Po Ku (Ch'in Pang-hsien), on the basis of a radiogram from Moscow, made the local decision to initiate the Long March. If these statements are true, it is noteworthy that Chou apparently survived Po Ku's fall from power and achieved added prominence during Mao's leadership.

After participating in the Long March, Chou served as the chief Communist representative in the negotiations leading to Chiang Kai-shek's release after the Sian kidnaping, and from that time forward he took part in nearly all important discussions between the Communists and the Kuomintang. More recently, he worked closely with Mao and Stalin in negotiating the Sino-Soviet Treaty of 1950.

It is extremely difficult to place Chou En-lai in any left-right spectrum of Chinese Communist politics. Through various shifts of the Communist line, he has been labeled leftist, rightist, and moderate, according to the stand he has taken toward the issues involved. It is said that he has great power, but prefers to exercise it through Mao, rather than in an independent fashion. Some observers consider him a likely successor to Mao, maintaining that he has a pwerful personal following, including Chu Te, P'eng Te-huai, Chen Yi, and Liu Po-ch'eng on the military side, and men like Tung Pi-wu and Ch'en Yün on the political; but there is no incontrovertible evidence to support this view.

When non-Communist observers discuss top figures in the Chinese Communist hierarchy and suggest possible successors to Mao Tse-tung, the name of Liu Shao-ch'i is nearly always mentioned. Like Mao, this important leader was born in Hunan of well-to-do peasant stock, studied at Hunan Normal School, and attended Peking University. Unlike Mao, he studied economics in the Soviet Union. After joining the Chinese Communist Party in 1921, he worked with Li Li-san as a union organizer among Anyuan miners, and with Mao in Hunan. In 1927 he was elected to the Central Committee of the Party. After the Communist-Kuomintang split of that year, he served at various times in the Manchurian labor movement and in the Shanghai underground.

Despite the fact that Liu Shao-ch'i reportedly supported Li Li-san during the period of urban insurrection, he was elected to the Politburo and the Secretariat in 1931, and is now believed to be loyal to Mao. After participating in the Long March, he was appointed Commissioner of Labor for the Shensi-Kansu-Ningsia Border Region Government in 1937. At the Seventh Congress of the Chinese Communist Party in 1945 he was elected vice-chairman of the Central Committee, and since then has been mentioned many times as Number Two man in the hierarchy and as Mao's most likely successor.

A veteran Bolshevik with thirty years of Party service, Liu is one of the more outstanding Communist scholars and Marxist-Leninist theoreticians that China has produced. In addition to such authoritative Chinese Communist works as On Intra-Party Struggle, The Training of the Party Member, and Internationalism and Nationalism, he is the author of On the Party, which possibly stands next to Mao's On the New Democracy as a guide for Chinese Communist theory and action. His prestige as a theoretician has spread throughout the Communist world, and in recent years certain of his pronouncements have been accepted as policy statements for the Communist line in Asia. It is entirely possible, however, that Liu Shao-ch'i will remain more a scholar than a man of action.

If this sketchy analysis of important individual Communists leaves unanswered all the leading questions about the capabilities, inclinations, and personal power relationships of Party leadership, it is simply an indication of how little we actually know about the Chinese Communist elite. In general, it is safe only to reiterate conclusions reached in the quantitative sections of this study, namely, that the top ranks of the Chinese Communist elite consist almost wholly of experienced, disciplined men, nearly all of whom have had twenty years or more of active, varied, and rigorous experience within the Communist movement.

The Chinese People's Republic

The Chinese Communist Party, by the middle of 1949, had won control over such vast areas of China that the decision was made to convene a new Political Consultative Conference. A Preparatory Committee composed of 134 delegates representing twenty-three organizations met in Peking June

15–20, 1949. This committee elected a twenty-one member Standing Committee, which, in turn, elected a chairman and five vice-chairmen. As an organizational forerunner of the Central People's Government of China inaugurated four months later, this Preparatory Committee is worthy of brief analysis.

Among the 133 delegates who actually attended (one did not attend), only twenty-five—or 18 percent—were known Communists. But since a sizable percentage of delegates about whom no information is available may also have been Communists, it is possible that the total may have been close to one-third of the attendance. The Democratic League with thirty-eight members had the largest representation (27 percent). The rest of the known membership consisted of eighteen members of the Kuomintang Revolutionary Committeemen, ten "non-partisans," and five Chih-kung Tang.[106]

The Standing Committee was one-third Communist, and most of the key positions were held by Reds—the chairman, one out of five vice-chairmen, the chief secretary of the Standing Committee, and chairmen of three out of six subcommittees.

The average age of the Preparatory Committee was fifty-two years. The average for non-Communist members was fifty-five years; for Communist members the average was fifty years.

More Committeemen were natives of Chekiang than any other province. Among Communists, however, Hunan (6 out of 25) and Kiangsu (5 out of 25) were the most common birthplaces. There is information concerning the educational backgrounds of 75 of the 133 Preparatory Committeemen: 28 were educated in China; 19 in Japan; 13 in the U.S.S.R.; 12 in France; 9 in the United States; and 5 in Germany. All but one of those educated in the Soviet Union and half of those who had received all or part of their training in France were members of the Communist Party.

The list of Committeemen includes the names of most Kuomintang (and other non-Communist) "liberals" who had been prominent since the end of the Japanese War and one well-known ex-Communist (T'an P'ing-shan) who had been expelled from the Party on the basis of Bolshevik discipline. When the State Administrative Council of the Central People's Government was announced on October 20, 1949, it was evident that the Chinese Communist Party had obtained an even stronger position in this body than it had enjoyed on the Preparatory Committee. This time out of 135 major posts,[107] more than half (70, or 51 percent) were held by known Communists.

Of the 21 Portfolio Ministries, 11 were headed by Communists. Of the 43 Vice-Ministers of the 21 Portfolios, 27 were Communist Party members. None of the Portfolio Ministries was staffed by non-Communists exclusively. Among 16 positions on the 4 committees, 8 were held by Communist Party members, and 2 of the committees were chaired by Communists. Of 16 commissions, 6 (out of 13) posts were held by Communists. Of the 4 administrations (Maritime Customs, News Agencies, Publications, and Information), 3 were headed by Communists, and among a total of 9 posts, 4 were held by Communists. The People's Bank had two responsible

officers, a director and a vice-director. Both were Communists. The
Academy of Sciences had a president and 4 vice-presidents. Two vice-
presidents were Communists. In nearly every case where a responsible
official was a non-Communist, his deputy was a recognized Communist,
and many of the prominent non-Communist members of the Council (such
as Mme. Liao Chung-k'ai; Mme. Feng Yü-hsiang, and Chang Po-chün)
had long records of support of, or long association with, the Chinese Communist movement.

On lower bureaucratic levels the percentage of Communist, as compared with non-Communist, officials necessarily diminished. It is often
said, in fact, that the Communist leadership, because its numbers are so
small in relation to the size and population of China, has already "spread
itself thin." The implication is, of course, that reliance upon untrained
personnel and upon Kuomintang bureaucrats insensitive to Communist
doctrine must seriously hamper Governmental functioning. There is truth
in this. But it is equally true that those absorbed by the new Government
include not only reluctant officials who had no other choice, but also
many able men who, through dissatisfaction with the Nationalist regime,
willingly transferred their allegiance. Many of these have been trained
in the West, and in time they will be joined by younger men who are now
attending institutions in the United States and Europe. Whether such persons render loyal service to the Communist regime or become dissidents
and even revolutionaries depends not only upon the performance of the
new Government, but also upon the policy which the Chinese Communist
Party follows in regard to non-Party personnel.

At the present time, increases in the ratio of Communist over non-Communist leaders holding high-level positions in the new government elite
suggest that the power position of the non-Communists will not improve
beyond the absolute requirements of governmental functioning, and an
examination of the basic principles of Marxist-Leninist-Stalinist class
warfare makes such a conclusion nearly mandatory.

By the establishment of pyramiding units of local government, moreover, the Chinese Communists have developed a pattern of military-politi-
cal controls which places a near monopoly of local power in the hands of
an exceedingly small group of senior leaders. At this writing (June 1952),
the mainland of China is divided into seven principal administrative regions, with organs and functions subordinate, but similar, to those of the
central government. It is noteworthy, then, that top administrative positions on regional and central government levels display a frequent over-
lapping of personnel, with key posts being held by senior Party, government, and military personnel. "By virtue of this great concentration of
control," according to reliable analysts, "a relatively small number of
senior Communists, almost all of whom are members of the Central
Committee of the Party, do at the same time dominate the regional governmental and military hierarchies. This control, exercised through Party
organizations at the regional level, both discourages and prevents centri-

fugal tendencies from developing."[108] The same source estimates that a group numbering fewer than twenty individuals may control completely the political and military situation at the regional level in Communist China.

In view of this high degree of centralization, is there even a remote possibility that critically important contradictions or schisms can develop either within the People's Republic itself, or within the Party, or between sections of the Chinese Communist Party and Bolshevik leaders in Moscow? At this point, no answer can be more than a speculation, but it is probably safe to say that the long-range future of the Chinese Communist movement is likely to depend upon at least four factors: the efficiency of Communist control techniques over the Chinese populace; the degree to which Red leadership remains sensitive to the needs of the country (especially the peasantry) and is reasonably able to meet them; the status of relations between China and the Soviet Union, on the one hand, and China and the United States, on the other; and the relations between the U. S. S. R. and the United States in a two-power world.

Chinese Communist leaders have stated their totalitarian intentions many times through the years, and the opening paragraph of the Constitution of the Chinese Communist Party makes clear that although the task of the Party "in the present stage" is to struggle for the development of a "new democracy," the ultimate aim is the realization of Communism in China. To date the Chinese Communists have published no precise time-table for the completion of their "present stage," but in June 1950 Mao Tse-tung estimated that about three years would be needed to accomplish current phases of agrarian reform, to "readjustment" commerce and industry, and to effect necessary government economies. Thereafter, at some unspecified future date, when the "test of war and the test of land reform" were passed, the only remaining task, the carrying out of Bolshevik socialist reform throughout the nation, would be passed easily.

Mao Tse-tung has indicated more than once that the Chinese Communist Party will not hesitate to use both calculated alliances with and armed struggle against the middle classes. During 1950 Chinese Communist leaders have published action programs defining principles and procedures for applying this kind of dual policy to industrial and agrarian problems. For this particular stage the Communist-controlled government will protect the interests of "all capitalists who benefit the nation's welfare and the people's livelihood" and for the time being will allow the rich peasants to maintain themselves. But the Chinese Communist radio, broadcasting about the trials and executions of "people's enemies," should remind us that "the existence and development of the Chinese Communist Party are inseparable from armed struggle."

Despite totalitarian methods, the Chinese Communist hierarchy, if it remains willing and able to adjust its doctrine to fundamental Chinese needs, may well remain in power a long time. If, on the other hand, it allows itself to become the mechanical instrument of Russo-Marxist dialectic and especially if it moves rapidly to force the peasant revolution into "higher" doctrinaire stages of Stalinist development, the Chinese Communist elite may run the risk of becoming a counterrevolutionary force in a new peasant upsurge.

Under either set of conditions, the record of Communist Party growth, of Russian misunderstandings and miscalculations in regard to the Chinese revolution, and of historic Chinese-Russian relations in and outside the Communist movement suggest that, in the long run, antagonisms between Chinese and Russian centers of Communism are almost certain to appear, if they are not already developing. Whether such antagonisms become critically disruptive or not may depend as much upon Western skill at exploiting them as upon Moscow-Peiping relations. In the meantime, Russian Communists, while helping the Chinese to improve their economy and to strengthen their military and political power, are likely to use Leninist-Stalinist techniques for tightening Russian discipline over the Chinese Communist movement, for achieving a Soviet-style penetration of China's economy and politics, and for preventing antagonisms from developing toward a crisis.

APPENDIX A. DEVELOPMENT OF THE KUOMINTANG

Chih-fang Wu (T. F. Wu), Chinese Government
and Politics (Shanghai, 1935) pp. 276–87

Hsingchunghui, or Society for the Regeneration of China, 1893–1905

T'ungmenghui, or Alliance Society, 1905–12

Kuomintang, or Nationalist Party, 1912–14

Chunghua Ko-mintang, or China Revolutionary Party, 1914–19

Chunghua Kuomintang, or Nationalist Party of China, 1920

Reorganization of the Chungkuo Kuomintang, 1924

APPENDIX B. KUOMINTANG ELITE

TABLE 1. CEC OF THE KUOMINTANG,* 1924

China Year Book 1931, p. 544

1. Chang Ching-chiang
2. Chou Lu (Tsou Lu)
3. Chü Cheng
4. En-Ke-Pa-T'u
5. Hsiung K'e-wu
6. Hu Han-min
7. Li Lieh-chün
8. Li Shou-chang
9. Liao Chung-k'ai
10. Lin Shen
11. Po Wen-wei
12. Shih Ching-yang
13. Shih Ying
14. Tai Chi-t'ao
15. T'an Cheng
16. T'an P'ing-shan
17. T'an Yen-k'ai
18. Ting Wei-fen
19. Wang Ching-wei
20. Wang Fa-ch'in
21. Yang Hsi-min
22. Yeh Ch'u-ts'ang
23. Yu Shu-te
24. Yü Yu-jen

*According to Chinese Communist Party histories, Li Ta-chao and Kan Shu-te, Communists, were among the twenty-four members of this Central Executive Committee.

TABLE 2. CEC OF THE KUOMINTANG, 1926

China Year Book 1931, p. 544

1. Ch'en Kung-po* (Communist or former Communist)
2. Ch'en Yu-jen* (Eugene Chen)
3. Ch'eng Ch'ien*
4. Chiang Kai-shek* (Chiang Chieh-shih)
5. Ching Heng-yi*
6. Chu Chi-hsün*
7. Chu P'ei-te*
8. En-Ke-Pa-T'u
9. Hsiao Fu-ch'eng*
10. Hsü Chien* (George Hsu)
11. Hu Han-min
12. Kan Nai-kuang*
13. Ku Meng-yü*
14. Li Chi-shen*
15. Li Lieh-chün
16. Li Shou-chang
17. Mme. Liao Chung-k'ai* (Ho Hsiang-ning)
18. Lin Tsu-han* (Communist)
19. Liu Shou-chung*
20. P'eng Che-ming* (Communist "allegiance")
21. Po Wen-wei
22. Sun Fo* (Sun K'o)
23. Sung Ch'ing-ling* (Mme. Sun Yat-sen)
24. Sung Tzu-wen* (T. V. Soong)
25. Tai Chi-t'ao
26. T'an P'ing-shan (Communist)
27. T'an Yen-k'ai
28. Ting Wei-fen
29. Wang Ching-wei
30. Wang Fa-ch'in
31. Wu Chao-shu*
32. Wu Yü-chang* (Communist)
33. Yang Pan-an* (Communist)
34. Yu Shu-te (Communist)
35. Yü Yu-jen
36. Yün Tai-ying* (Communist)

* Newly elected in 1926.

TABLE 3. CEC OF THE KUOMINTANG, 1929

[The China Weekly Review, XLVIII, No. 5 (March 30, 1929), 213]

1. Chang Ch'ün*
2. Chao Tai-wen*
3. Ch'en Chao-ying*
4. Ch'en Kuo-fu*
5. Ch'en Li-fu*
6. Ch'en Ming-shu*
7. Chiang Kai-shek
   (Chiang Chieh-shih)
8. Chou Ch'i-kang*
9. Chu Chia-hua*
10. Chu P'ei-te
11. Fang Chen-wu*
12. Fang Chiao-hui*
13. Feng Yü-hsiang*
14. Ho Ch'eng-chün*
15. Ho Ying-ch'in*
16. Hu Han-min
17. Li Wen-fan*
18. Liu Chih* (Liu Shih)
19. Liu Chi-wen*
20. Liu Lu-ying
21. Shao Yüan-ch'ung*
22. Sun Fo (Sun K'o)
23. Sung Ch'ing-ling (Mme. Sun Yat-sen)
24. Sung Tzu-wen (T.V. Soong)
25. Tai Chi-t'ao
26. T'an Yen-k'ai
27. Ting Wei-fen
28. Tseng Yang-fu*
29. Wang Ching-wei
30. Wang Po-ling*
31. Wu Ch'ao-shu
32. Wu Te-chen* (Wu T'ieh-ch'eng)
33. Yang Shu-chuang*
34. Yeh Ch'u-ts'ang
35. Yen Hsi-shan*
36. Yü Yu-jen

*Newly elected in 1929.

TABLE 4. CEC OF THE KUOMINTANG, 1931

[China Year Book 1931, pp. 583–84]

1. Chang Chen*
2. Chang Ch'ün
3. Ch'en Chao-ying
4. Ch'en Kuo-fu
5. Ch'en Li-fu
6. Ch'en Ming-shu
7. Ch'en Yao-yuan*
8. Chiang Kai-shek (Chiang Chieh-shih)
9. Chou Ch'i-kang
10. Chu Chia-hua
11. Chu P'ei-te
12. Fang Chiao-hui
13. Ho Ch'eng-chün
14. Ho Ying-ch'in
15. Hu Han-min
16. K'ung Hsiang-hsi*
17. Li Wen-fan
18. Liu Chi-wen
19. Liu Lu-ying
20. Liu Shih (Liu Chih)
21. Shao Yüan-ch'ung
22. Sun Fo (Sun K'o)
23. Sung Ch'ing-ling (Mme. Sun Yat-sen)
24. Sung Tzu-wen (T.V. Soong)
25. Tai Chi-t'ao
26. Ting Ch'ao-wu*
27. Ting Wei-fen
28. Tseng Yang-fu
29. Wang Cheng-t'ing*
30. Wang Po-ch'ün*
31. Wang Po-ling
32. Wu Ch'ao-shu
33. Wu T'ieh-ch'eng (Wu Te-chen)
34. Yang Shu-chuang
35. Yeh Ch'u-ts'ang
36. Yü Yu-jen

*Newly elected in 1931.

TABLE 5. CEC OF THE KUOMINTANG, 1931

[The Chinese Year Book, 1935–36, p. 147]

1. Chang Chen
2. Chang Chih-pen
3. Chang Ch'ün
4. Chang Hui-chang
5. Chao Tai-wen
6. Ch'en Chao-ying
7. Ch'en Chi-t'ang
8. Ch'en Kung-po
9. Ch'en Kuo-fu
10. Ch'en Li-fu
11. Ch'en Ts'e
12. Ch'eng Ch'ien
13. Chiang Kai-shek
14. Ching Heng-yi
15. Chou Ch'i-kang
16. Chou Fo-hai
17. Chü Cheng
18. Chu Chia-hua
19. Chu P'ei-te
20. Fang Chiao-hui
21. Feng Yü-hsiang
22. Fu Ju-lin
23. Ho Ch'eng-chün
24. Ho Hsiang-ning (Mme. Liao Chung-k'ai
25. Ho Yao-chu
26. Ho Ying-ch'in
27. Hsia Tou-yin
28. Hsiung K'e-wu
29. Hu Han-min
30. Kan Nai-kuang
31. Ku Chu-t'ung
32. Ku Meng-yü
33. Kuei Ch'ung-chi
34. K'ung Hsiang-hsi
35. Li Lieh-chün
36. Li Tsung-huang
37. Li Wen-fan
38. Li Yang-ching
39. Lin Yi-chung
40. Liu Chih (Liu Shih)
41. Liu Chi-wen
42. Liu Lu-ying
43. Liu Shou-chung
44. Ma Ch'ao-chün
45. Mao Tsu-ch'üan
46. Po Ch'ung-hsi
47. Po Wen-wei
48. Po Yün-t'i
49. Shao Yüan-ch'ung
50. Shih Ching-yang
51. Shih Ying
52. Sun Fo (Sun K'o)
53. Sung Ch'ing-ling
54. Sung Tzu-wen
55. Tai Chi-t'ao
56. T'an Cheng
57. Teng Chia-yen
58. Ting Ch'ao-wu
59. Ting Wei-fen
60. Tseng Yang-fu
61. Wang Cheng-t'ing (C. T. Wang)
62. Wang Ching-wei
63. Wang Fa-ch'in
64. Wang Po-ch'ün
65. Wang Po-ling
66. Wu Te-chen (Wu T'ieh-ch'eng)
67. Yang Chieh
68. Yeh Ch'u-ts'ang
69. Yen Hsi-shan
70. Yü Han-mou
71. Yü Yu-jen

TABLE 6. CEC OF THE KUOMINTANG, 1935

China Weekly Review, XXIV (November 30, 1934), 453

1. Chang Chih-chung*
2. Chang Ch'ün
3. Chang Chung *
4. Chang Hsüeh-liang*
5. Chang Li-sheng*
6. Chang Tao-fan*
7. Chao Tai-wen
8. Ch'en Chao-ying
9. Ch'en Ch'eng*
10. Ch'en Chi-ch'eng*
11. Ch'en Chi-t'ang*
12. Ch'en Kung-po
13. Ch'en Kuo-fu
14. Ch'en Li-fu
15. Ch'en Pu-lei*
16. Ch'en Shao-k'uan*
17. Ch'en Ts'e*
18. Ch'en Yi* (Ch'en I)
19. Cheng Chan-nan*
20. Chiang Kai-shek (Chiang Chieh-shih)
21. Chiang Po-ch'eng*
22. Chiang Ting-wen*
23. Chiao I-t'ang*
24. Ch'ien Ta-chun*
25. Chou Ch'i-kang
26. Chou Fo-hai*
27. Chou Po-min*
28. Chü Cheng
29. Chu Chia-hua
30. Chu P'ei-te
31. Chu Shao-liang*
32. Fang Chiao-hui
33. Fang Chih*
34. Feng Yü-hsiang*
35. Fu Ping-ch'ang*
36. Fu Tso-yi*
37. Han Fu-ch'ü*
38. Ho Ch'eng-chün
39. Ho Chien*
40. Ho Chung-han*
41. Ho Ying-ch'in
42. Hsia Tou-yin*
43. Hsiao Chi-shan*
44. Hsiao T'ung-tz'u*
45. Hsiung Shih-hui*
46. Hsu En-tseng*
47. Hsü K'an*
48. Hsü Yüan-ch'üan*
49. Hu Han-min
50. Huang Hsü-ch'u*
51. Huang Mu-tung*
52. Hung Lan-yu*
53. Hung Lu-tung*
54. Kan Nai-kuang
55. Ku Cheng-kang*
56. Ku Cheng-lun*
57. Ku Chu-t'ung*
58. Ku Meng-yü
59. Kung-Chio-Chung-Ni*
60. K'ung Hsiang-hsi
61. Li Shen-ta*
62. Li Tsung-huang*
63. Li Wen-fan
64. Li Yang-ching*
65. Liang Han-ts'ao*
66. Lin Yi-chung*
67. Liu Chien-hsü*
68. Liu Chih (Liu Shih)
69. Liu Chi-wen
70. Liu Hsiang*
71. Liu Lu-ying
72. Liu Wei-chih*
73. Lo Ching-tao*
74. Lo-sang-chien-tsan*
75. Lu Chung-lin*
76. Ma Ch'ao-chün*
77. Mai-ssu-wu-te*
78. Mao Tsu-ch'üan*
79. Mei Kung-jen*
80. Miao P'ei-ch'eng*
81. Miao P'ei-nan*
82. P'an Kung-chan*
83. P'eng Hsüeh-p'ei*
84. Po Ch'ung-hsi*
85. Po Wen-wei

TABLE 6 (Continued)

86. Shen Hung-lieh*
87. Shih Ying
88. Sun Fo (Sun K'o)
89. Sung Tzu-wen (T. V. Soong)
90. Tai Chi-t'ao
91. Tai Huai-sheng*
92. T'ang Yu-jen*
93. T'ien K'un-shan*
94. Ting Ch'ao-wu
95. Ting Wei-fen
96. Tseng K'uo-ch'ing*
97. Tseng Yang-fu
98. Tsou Lu (Chou Lu)
99. Wang Chi*
100. Wang Ching-wei
101. Wang Chuan-sheng*
102. Wang Chun*
103. Wang Fa-ch'in

104. Wang I-che*
105. Wang Lu-yi*
106. Wang Po-ch'ün
107. Wang Po-ling
108. Wang Sou-fang*
109. Wei Li-huang*
110. Wu Hsing-ya*
111. Wu Te-chen (Wu T'ieh-ch'eng)
112. Yang Chieh*
113. Yeh Ch'u-ts'ang
114. Yen Hsi-shan
115. Yü Ching-t'ang*
116. Yü Han-mou*
117. Yu Hsi-shan*
118. Yü Hsüeh-chung*
119. Yü Yu-jen

*Newly elected in 1935.

TABLE 7. CEC OF THE KUOMINTANG, 1945

<u>Biographies</u> <u>of</u> <u>Kuomintang</u> <u>Leaders,</u> Harvard University, 1948

1. Chang Chen*
2. Chang Chia-ao*
3. Chang Ch'iang*
4. Chang Chih-chiang*
5. Chang Chih-chung
6. Chang Ch'ün
7. Chang Kuo-t'ao*
8. Chang Li-sheng
9. Chang Tao-fan
10. Chang T'ing-hsiu*
11. Chang Wei*
12. Chao Yün-yi*
13. Ch'en Chao-ying
14. Ch'en Ch'eng
15. Ch'en Chi-ch'eng
16. Ch'en Chi-t'ang
17. Ch'en Chien-ju*
18. Ch'en Ch'ing-yün*
19. Ch'en Fang-hsien*
20. Ch'en Hsi-hao*

21. Ch'en Hsüeh-p'ing*
22. Ch'en I (Ch'en Yi)
23. Ch'en Kuo-ch'u*
24. Ch'en Kuo-fu
25. Ch'en Li-fu
26. Ch'en Lien-fen*
27. Ch'en Pu-lei
28. Ch'en Shao-k'uan
29. Ch'en Shih-ch'üan*
30. Ch'en Shu-jen*
31. Ch'en Ts'e
32. Cheng Chieh-min*
33. Ch'eng Ch'ien
34. Ch'eng Ssu-yüan*
35. Ch'eng T'ien-fang*
36. Cheng Yen-fen*
37. Ch'i Shih-ying*
38. Chiang Po-ch'eng
39. Chiang Ting-wen
40. Chiao I-t'ang

TABLE 7 (Continued)

41. Ch'ien Ta-chün
42. Chou Ch'i-kang
43. Chou Chih-jou*
44. Chou Po-min
45. Chou Yi-pin*
46. Chü Cheng
47. Chu Chi-ch'ing*
48. Chu Chia-hua
49. Chu Huai-ping*
50. Chu Shao-liang
51. Fan Yü-sui*
52. Fang Chiao-hui
53. Fang Chih
54. Fang Ch'ing-ju*
55. Feng Ch'in-tsai*
56. Feng Yü-hsiang
57. Fu Ju-lin*
58. Fu Ping-ch'ang
59. Fu Tso-yi
60. Han Chen-sheng*
61. Ho Ch'eng-chün
62. Ho Chien
63. Ho Chung-han
64. Ho Ying-ch'in
65. Hsia Tou-yin
66. Hsia Wei*
67. Hsiang Chuan-yi*
68. Hsiang Ting-jung*
69. Hsiao Cheng*
70. Hsiao Chi-shan
71. Hsiao T'ung-tz'u
72. Hsiung Shih-hui
73. Hsü Chen*
74. Hsü K'an
75. Hsü Shao-ti*
76. Hsü Yüan-ch'üan
77. Hsüeh Tu-pi*
78. Hu Ch'ien-chung*
79. Hu Tsung-nan*
80. Huang Chi-lu*
81. Huang Chung-hsiang*
82. Huang Hsü-ch'u
83. Huang Shih*
84. Huang Yü-jen*
85. Hung Lan-yu
86. Hung Lu-tung
87. Jo Chen*
88. Kan Chia-hsing*
89. Kan Nai-kuang
90. K'ang Tse*
91. Ku Cheng-kang
92. Ku Cheng-lun
93. Ku Cheng-ting*
94. Ku Chu-t'ung
95. Ku Hsi-p'ing*
96. Ku Meng-yü
97. Ku Wei-chün* (V.K. Wellington Koo)
98. Kuan Lin-cheng*
99. Kuei Yung-ch'ing*
100. K'ung Hsiang-hsi
101. Kung Tzu-chih*
102. Kuo Hsien*
103. Lai Lien*
104. Li Chung-hsiang*
105. Li Han-hun*
106. Li I-chung*
107. Li Jen-jen*
108. Li Mo-an*
109. Li P'ei-chi*
110. Li P'in-hsien*
111. Li Shu-hua*
112. Li Ta-chao*
113. Li Tsung-huang
114. Li Wei-kuo*
115. Li Wen-fan
116. Li Yang-ching
117. Liang Han-ts'ao
118. Lin Hsüeh-yüan*
119. Lin Tieh*
120. Lin Yi-chung
121. Liu Chien-ch'ün*
122. Liu Chien-hsü
123. Liu Chih (Liu Shih)
124. Liu Chi-hung*
125. Liu Chi-wen
126. Liu Fei*
127. Liu K'o-shu*

TABLE 7 (Continued)

128. Liu Wei-chih
129. Liu Wen-hui*
130. Liu Yao-chang*
131. Lo Chia-lun*
132. Lo Cho-ying*
133. Lo Mei-huan*
134. Lo Sha-t'ien*
135. Lo-sang-chien-tsan
136. Lou T'ung-sun*
137. Lu Ch'ung-jen*
138. Lu Chung-lin
139. Lu Fu-t'ing*
140. Lu Han*
141. Lü Yün-chang*
142. Ma Ch'ao-chün
143. Ma Hung-k'uei*
144. Ma Yüan-fang*
145. Mai-ssu-wu-te
146. Mao Tsu-ch'üan
147. Mei Kung-jen
148. Mei Yi-ch'i*
149. Mei Yu-cho*
150. Miao P'ei-ch'eng
151. Miao P'ei-nan
152. Ou-yang Chü*
153. P'an Kung-chan
154. P'an Kung-pi*
155. P'ang Ching-t'ang*
156. P'eng Chao-hsien*
157. P'eng Hsüeh-p'ei
158. Po Ch'ung-hsi
159. Po Wen-wei
160. Po Yün-t'i*
161. Shen Hui-lien*
162. Shen Hung-lieh
163. Shih Tzu-chou*
164. Sun Fo (Sun K'o)
165. Sun Wei-ju*
166. Sung Ch'ing-ling (Mme. Sun Yat-sen)
167. Sung Hsi-lien*
168. Sung Mei-ling* (Mme. Chiang Kai-shek)
169. Sung Tzu-wen (T. V. Soong)
170. Ta-li-cha-ya*
171. Tai Ch'uan-hsien (Tai Chi-t'ao)
172. Tai Huai-sheng
173. T'ang En-po*
174. T'ang Sheng-chih*
175. Teng Chia-yen*
176. Teng Fei-huang*
177. Teng Hsi-hou*
178. Teng Pao-shan*
179. Teng Wen-yi*
180. Ti Ying*
181. T'ien K'un-shan*
182. Ting Ch'ao-wu
183. Ting Wei-fen
184. Tseng K'uo-ch'ing
185. Tseng Yang-fu
186. Tsou Lu (Chou Lu)
187. Tuan Hsi-p'eng*
188. Tung Hsien-kuang* (Hollington Tong)
189. Wan Fu-lin*
190. Wang Cheng-t'ing
191. Wang Ch'i-chiang*
192. Wang Ling-chi*
193. Wang Mou-kung*
194. Wang Tsan-hsü*
195. Wang Tsung-shan*
196. Wang Tung-yüan*
197. Wang Yao-wu*
198. Wei Li-huang
199. Wei Tao-ming*
200. Weng Wen-hao*
201. Wu Chung-hsin*
202. Wu I-feng*
203. Wu K'ai-hsien*
204. Wu Pao-feng*
205. Wu Shang-ying*
206. Wu Shao-shu*
207. Wu T'ieh-ch'eng (Wu Te-chen)
208. Yang Ai-yüan*‡
209. Yang Chieh
210. Yang Tuan-liu*

TABLE 7 (Continued)

211. Yeh Ch'u-ts'ang
212. Yeh Hsiu-feng*
213. Yen Hsi-shan
214. Yen Hua-t'ang*
215. Yü Ching-t'ang
216. Yü Chün-hsien*
217. Yü Fei-peng*

218. Yü Han-mou
219. Yü Hsüeh-chung
220. Yü Hung-chün*
221. Yü Yu-jen
222. Yüan Shou-ch'ien*
223. Yüan Yung (?)* ‡

*Newly elected in 1945.

‡The 1945 Year Book names all but Yang Ai-yüan and Yüan Yung. Chiang Kai-shek as Tsungtsai is not included.

APPENDIX C. COMMUNIST PARTY ELITE

TABLE 1. CONGRESSES OF THE CHINESE COMMUNIST PARTY

Congress	Date		Place	Number of Delegates	Reported Party Membership
First	July	1921	Shanghai	13	50
Second	May	1922	West Lake, Hangchow	20	100
Third	June	1923	Canton	20	300
Fourth	January	1925	Shanghai	—	1,000 (at least)
Fifth	April	1927	Hankow	100	60,000
Special	August	1927	Kiukiang	22	
Sixth	August	1928	Moscow	50	15,000
Seventh	April	1945	Yenan	485	1,000,000 (or more)

TABLE 2. DELEGATES TO THE FIRST CHINESE COMMUNIST PARTY CONGRESS*

(July 1921)

The information in the following table was drawn from Kanichi Hatano, History of the Chinese Communist Party, Asia Mondai Koza, Vol. II, Tokyo, 1936; History of the Chinese Communist Party, Japanese Foreign Office, July 1931; Chung-kuo hsien-tui ko-ming yun-tung shih, 1941, Hsin-hua shu-tien, Chap. V, Sec. 2, "The Birth of the Communist Party"; Edgar Snow, Red Star over China, p. 157.

Name	Representing	Fate
1. Chang Kuo-t'ao	Peking	Alive March 15, 1950
2. Ch'en Kung-po	Kwangtung	Executed June 4, 1948
3. Ch'en T'an-ch'iu	Wuhan	Alive January 1, 1950
4. Chou Fo-hai	Japan	Died in prison February 28, 1948
5. Ho Shu-heng	Changsha	Shot in May 1934 by KMT
6. Li Han-chün	Shanghai	Killed by KMT in 1927
7. Li Ta	Shanghai	Uncertain. A "Li Ta" was alive January 15, 1949
8. Liu Jen-ch'ing	Peking	Uncertain
9. Mao Tse-tung	Changsha	Alive March 15, 1950
10. Pao Hui-seng	Kwangtung	Alive March 15, 1950
11. T'ien En-min		Uncertain
12. Tung Pi-wu	Wuhan	Alive March 15, 1950
13. Wang Ch'iu-meng		Uncertain

*Tentative list.

It is probable that Comintern representatives Voitinsky and Maring were also present although, according to some reports, Voitinsky was not there, but Maring and another agent named Nikorusky.

TABLE 3. POLITBURO: CCP*

(Fifth Congress, April 1927)

Chang Kuo-t'ao
Ch'en Tu-hsiu†
Chou En-lai†
Ch'ü Ch'iu-pai†
Li Li-san†

Li Wei-han†
T'an P'ing-shan†
Su Chao-cheng†
Ts'ai Ho-shen†

*Tentative list.
†New members.

TABLE 4. POLITBURO: CCP*

(Reorganized July 13, 1927)

Chang T'ai-lei†
Ch'in Pang-hsien†
Chou En-lai
Ch'ü Ch'iu-pai

Li Wei-han
P'eng P'ai†
Su Chao-cheng

*Tentative list. Sources differ as to whether or not Mao was a full member of this Politburo.
†New members.

TABLE 5. "RULING CLIQUE": CCP*

(August 7, 1927)

Chou En-lai
Ch'ü Ch'iu-pai
Hsiang Chung-fa†

Li Li-san
Li Wei-han
Liu Shao-ch'i†

*Tentative list.
†New members.

TABLE 6. POLITBURO: CCP*

(Sixth Congress, July-September, 1928)

Chang Kuo-t'ao
Chou En-lai
Ch'ü Ch'iu-pai
Hsiang Chung-fa (Sec. Gen.)

Hu Wen-chiang†
Li Li-san
Ts'ai Ho-shen

*Tentative list. This list may or may not be complete.
†New member.

TABLE 7. POLITBURO: CCP*

(Fourth Plenum, January 8, 1931)

Chang Wen-t'ien†   Chou En-lai
Ch'en Shao-yü†   Hsiang Chung-fa (Sec. Gen.)
Ch'in Pang-hsien (?)   Shen Tse-min†

* Tentative list. This list is probably incomplete.
† New members.

TABLE 8. POLITBURO: CCP*

(June 1931)

Chang Wen-t'ien   Chou En-lai
Ch'en Shao-yü (Sec. Gen.)   Meng Ch'ing-shu (Mme.
Ch'in Pang-hsien   Ch'en Shao-yü)†
                                   Shen Tse-min

*Tentative list. This list may or may not be complete.
†New member.

TABLE 9. POLITBURO: CCP*

(January 1934)

Chang Wen-t'ien   Liang Pai-tai†
Ch'en Shao-yü   Liu Shao-ch'i
Ch'in Pang-hsien   Mao Tse-tung
Chou En-lai   Wang Chia-hsiang†
Chu Te†   Wu Liang-ping†
Hsiang Ying†

*Tentative list.
†New members.

TABLE 10. POLITBURO: CCP*

(April-July, 1937)

Chang Kuo-t'ao   Chu Te
Chang Wen-t'ien   Mao Tse-tung
Ch'in Pang-hsien   Wang Chia-hsiang
Chou En-lai

*Tentative list. This list is probably incomplete.

TABLE 11. POLITBURO: CCP*

(Post-1945)

Chang Wen-t'ien
Ch'en Yün[†]
Chou En-lai
Chu Te
Jen Pi-shih[†]
K'ang Sheng[†]
Kao Kang[†]

Lin Tsu-han[†]
Liu Shao-ch'i
Mao Tse-tung
P'eng Chen[†]
Tung Pi-wu
Wang Chia-hsiang

*Tentative list.
[†]New members.

TABLE 12. POLITBURO: CCP*

(November 15, 1951)
Current Background, No. 137, American Consulate General,
Hong Kong, p. 5

Ch'en Yün
Chou En-lai
Chu Te
Lin Tsu-han

Liu Shao-ch'i (Deputy Chairman)
Mao Tse-tung (Chairman)
P'eng Chen

TABLE 13. CENTRAL COMMITTEE OF THE CHINESE COMMUNIST PARTY (1945)*

China Digest, July 13, 1949, p. 17

1. Chang Ting-ch'eng
2. Chang Yün-yi
3. Ch'en Shao-yü (Wang Ming)
4. Ch'en T'an-ch'iu
5. Ch'en Yi
6. Ch'en Yün
7. Cheng Wei-san
8. Ch'in Pang-hsien (Po Ku)
   (Wang Chia-hsiang 2/15/50)[†]
9. Chou En-lai
10. Chu Te
11. Ho Lung
12. Hsu Hsiang-ch'ien
13. Hsü T'e-li
14. Jao Shu-shih

15. Jen Pi-shih
16. K'ang Sheng
17. Kao Kang
18. Kuan Hsiang-ying (Liao Ch'eng-chih, 2/15/50)[†]
19. Li Fu-ch'un
20. Li Hsien-nien
21. Li Li-san
22. Lin Feng
23. Lin Piao
24. Lin Po-ch'ü (Lin Tsu-han)
25. Liu Po-ch'eng
26. Liu Shao-ch'i
27. Lo Fu (Chang Wen-t'ien)
28. Lo Jung-huan

TABLE 13   (Continued)

29. Lo Ting-yi (Lu Ting-yi)	37. T'eng Tai-yüan
30. Mao Tse-tung	38. Teng Tzu-hui
31. Nieh Jung-chen	39. Ts'ai Ch'ang (Miss)
32. P'eng Chen	40. Tseng Shan
33. P'eng Te-huai	41. Tung Pi-wu
34. Po Yi-p'o	42. Wang Jo-fei (Ch'en Po-ta,
35. T'an Chen-lin	2/15/50)†
36. Teng Shiu-ping (Teng	43. Wu Yü-chang
Hsiao-p'ing)	44. Yeh Chien-ying

*Tentative list.

† As of February 15, 1950, the Central Committee included the same members, except that Ch'in Pang-hsien, Kuan Hsiang-ying, and Wang Jo-fei, who have died since 1945, were replaced by Wang Chia-hsiang, Liao Ch'eng-chih, and Ch'en Po-ta.

In 1945 the top six alternates, in order, were Liao Ch'eng-chih, Wang Chia-hsiang, Ch'en Po-ta, Wang Shou-tao, Li Yu, and Teng Ying-ch'ao.

TABLE 14. CENTRAL COMMITTEE OF THE CHINESE COMMUNIST PARTY*

(November 15, 1951)
Current Background, No. 137, American Consulate General
Hong Kong, p. 3

1. Mao Tse-tung	13. Lo Jung-huan
2. Chu Te	14. K'ang Sheng
3. Liu Shao-ch'i	15. P'eng Chen
Jen Pi-shih (deceased)	Wang Jo-fei (deceased)
4. Lin Tsu-han (Lin Po ch'ü)	16. Chang Yün-yi
5. Lin Piao	17. Ho Lung
6. Tung Pi-wu	18. Ch'en Yi
7. Ch'en Yün	19. Chou En-lai
8. Hsu Hsiang-ch'ien	20. Liu Po-ch'eng
Kuan Hsiang-ying (deceased), Ch'en T'an-ch'iu (deceased)	21. Cheng Wei-san
	22. Chang Wen-t'ien (Lo Fu)
9. Kao Kang	23. Ts'ai Ch'ang (Mme. Li
10. Li Fu-ch'un	Fu-ch'un)
11. Jao Shu-shih	24. Teng Hsiao-p'ing
12. Li Li-san	25. Lu Ting-yi
	26. Tseng Shan

TABLE 14 (Continued)

27. Yeh Chien-ying
28. Nieh Jung-chen
29. P'eng Te-huai
30. Teng Tzu-hui
31. Wu Yü-chang
32. Lin Feng
33. T'eng Tai-yüan
34. Chang Ting-ch'eng
35. Hsü T'e-li

36. T'an Chen-lin
37. Li Hsien-nien
38. Po Yi-p'o
39. Ch'en Shao-yü
    Ch'in Pang-hsien (deceased)
40. Liao Ch'eng-chih
41. Wang Chia-hsiang
42. Ch'en Po-ta
43. Huang K'o-ch'eng†

*Arranged in the order of votes received

†Huang K'o-ch'eng is the only member not on the previous list.

TABLE 1. BASIC DATA ON POLITBURO MEMBERS

Group	Number of Members	Average Age	Birthplace	Education	Father's Status	Father's General Occupation	Class
Delegates 1st Congress (Ch'en incl.) July 1921	14	29.4 (Don't know, 5)	Hunan 3, Hupeh 3, Kiangsi 1, Anhwei 1, Kwangtung 1 (Don't know, 5)	China 4, Japan 4, S.U. 3, U.S. 1 (Don't know, 6)	Wealthy landlord 2, Wealthy peasant 1, Revolutionist 1 (Don't know, 10)	Landlord 2, Peasant 1, Scholar 1	Upper, upper-middle 3, Middle 0, Lower-middle, lower 1
Politburo April 1927	9	33.4 (Don't know, 2)	Hunan 3, Kiangsu 2, Kiangsi 1, Anhwei 1, Kwangtung 1 (Don't know, 1)	France 5, China 4, S.U. 4, Japan 2, Germany 1 (Don't know, 1)	Statesman 1, Mandarin 1, Wealthy landlord 1, Small merchant 1, Poor peasant 1 (Don't know, 4)	Landlord 1, Merchant 1, Peasant 1, Scholar-official 2	Upper-upper middle 3, Middle 0, Lower-middle, lower 2
Politburo July 13, 1927	7	27.3 (Don't know, 3)	Kiangsu 3, Hunan 1 (Don't know, 3)	S.U. 3, France 2, China 2, Japan 1, Germany 1 (Don't know, 3)	Statesman 1, Mandarin 1, Provincial governor 1, Landlord 1 (Don't know, 3)	Landlord 1, Scholar-official 3	Upper, upper-middle 4, Middle 0, Lower-middle, lower 0
"Ruling Clique" August 7, 1927	6	29.0 (Don't know, 1)	Hunan 3, Kiangsu 2, Hupeh 1	S.U. 5, France 3, China 3, Japan 1, Germany 1	Statesman 1, Mandarin 1, Wealthy peasant 1, Poor peasant 1, Boatman 1 (Don't know, 1)	Scholar-official 2, Peasant 2, Proletarian 1	Upper, upper-middle 2, Middle 0, Lower-middle, lower 3

Group	N	Average age	Province	Education (country)	Father's occupation	Class origin	Social class
Politburo (may be complete), July-September, 1928	7	30.0 (Don't know, 3)	Hunan 2, Kiangsu 2, Hupeh 1, Kiangsi 1 (Don't know, 1)	S.U. 5, France 3, China 3, Japan 1, Germany 1 (Don't know, 1)	Statesman 1, Mandarin 1, Wealthy landlord 1, Poor peasant 1, Boatman 1 (Don't know, 2)	Landlord 1, Peasant 1, Scholar-official 1, Proletarian 1	Upper, upper-middle 3, Middle 0, Lower-middle, lower 2
Politburo (probably incomplete), January 8, 1931	6	29.0 (Don't know, 2)	Kiangsu 3, Anhwei 1, Hupeh 1 (Don't know, 1)	S.U. 5, France 1, Japan 1, Germany 1, U.S. 1 (Don't know, 1)	Mandarin 1, Provincial governor 1, Wealthy peasant 2, Boatman 1 (Don't know, 1)	Peasant 1, Scholar-official 1, Proletarian 1	Upper, upper-middle 2, Middle 0, Lower-middle, lower 3
Politburo (may be complete), June 1931	6	28.4 (Don't know, 1)	Kiangsu 3, Anhwei 2 (Don't know, 1)	S.U. 5, China 2, France 1, Japan 1, Germany 1, U.S. 1 (Don't know, 1)	Mandarin 1, Provincial governor 1, Wealthy peasant 2 (Don't know, 2)	Scholar-official 1, Peasant 1	Upper, upper-middle 3, Middle 0, Lower-middle, lower 2 (Don't know, 1)
Politburo January 1934	11	35.2 (Don't know, 1)	Kiangsu 3, Hunan 2, Anhwei 2, Hupeh 1, Szechwan 1, Chekiang 1 (Don't know, 1)	S.U. 8, China 6, France 2, Germany 2, Japan 1, U.S. 1, No education 1 (Don't know, 1)	Mandarin 1, Provincial governor 1, Merchant 1, Wealthy peasant 4, Peasant 1, Landless peasant 1, Seamstress 1 (Don't know, 1)	Merchant 1, Peasant 6, Scholar-official 1, Proletarian 1	Upper, upper-middle 2, Middle 1, Lower-middle, lower 7

TABLE 1 (Continued)

Group	Number of Members	Average Age	Birthplace	Education	Father's Status	Father's General Occupation	Class
Politburo (probably incomplete), July 1937	7	39.3	Kiangsu, Hunan, Anhwei, Szechwan, Kiangsi	S.U. 3; China 1; France 1; Germany 1; Japan 1; U.S.	Mandarin 1; Provincial governor 1; Wealthy landlord 2; Wealthy peasant 1; Peasant 1; Landless peasant 1	Landlord 1; Peasant 4; Scholar-official 2	Upper, upper-middle 3; Middle 0; Lower-middle, lower 4
Politburo post-1945	13	48.9 (in 1945)	Hunan, Kiangsu, Anhwei, Hupeh, Szechwan, Shantung, Shensi, Shansi	S.U. 4; China 3; Japan 1; France 1; Germany 1; U.S. 1; No education 1	Mandarin 1; Wealthy landlord 2; Wealthy landlord official 1; Official 1; Wealthy peasant 1; Peasant 4; Landless peasant 2; (Don't know, 1)	Landlord 3; Peasant 7; Scholar-official 2	Upper, upper-middle 5; Middle 0; Lower-middle, lower 7

Total Polit-
buro Members   42   33.0

Hunan (8)	19.1
Hupeh (5)	11.9
Kiangsu(5)	11.9
Anhwei (4)	9.5
Kwangtung(2)	4.8
Kiangsi (1)	2.4
Szechwan(1)	2.4
Chekiang(1)	2.4
Shantung(1)	2.4
Shensi (1)	2.4
Shansi (1)	2.4
Don't know (12)	28.6
	100.0

Soviet Union(20)	47.6
China (13)	31.0
France (6)	14.3
Japan (5)	11.9
United States (2)	4.8
Germany(2)	4.8
None (2)	4.8
Don't know (13)	31.0
China and Russia only (18)	42.9
China only (2)†	4.8
Military (2)	4.8

Wealthy land-lord (3)	7.1
Wealthy land-lord offi-cial (1)	2.4
Landlord(1)	2.4
Mandarin (1)	2.4
Statesman (1)	2.4
Prov. Gov-ernor (1)	2.4
Official (1)	2.4
Revolution-ist (1)	2.4
Merchant(1)	2.4
Small Merch-ant (1)	2.4
Wealthy peas-ant (6)	14.3
Peasant (1)	2.4
Poor peas-ant (1)	2.4
Landless peasant (2)	4.8
Boatman(1)	2.4
Seamstress (1)	2.4
Don't know (18)	42.9
	100.0

Landlord (5)	11.9
Scholar-official(4)	9.5
Scholar (1)	2.4
Merch-ant (2)	4.8
Peasant (10)	23.8
Proletarian (2)	4.8
Don't know (18)	42.9
	100.0

Upper, upper-middle(11)	26.2
Middle (1)	2.4
Lower-middle, lower(13)	31.0
Don't know (17)	40.5
	100.0

*Average of the ten Committees.
† Mao Tse-tung and T'an P'ing-shan.

TABLE 2. BASIC DATA ON CENTRAL COMMITTEE, CCP, 1945

Age

Average age	46.8
Oldest	68
Youngest	36
66–70	2 members
61–65	0
56–60	3
51–55	3
46–50	14
41–45	14
36–40	7
Don't know	1
Total	44

Father's Status

	No.	Percent
Aristocrat	2	4.6
Upper class	1	2.3
Wealthy landlord	7	15.9
Provincial governor	1	2.3
Wealthy merchant	1	2.3
Merchant	1	2.3
Small landlord	1	2.3
Middle class	3	6.8
Wealthy peasant	6	13.6
Peasant	1	2.3
Poor peasant	4	9.1
Proletariat	2	4.6
Don't know	14	31.8

Birthplace

	No.	Percent
Hunan	(12)	27.3
Szechwan	(6)	13.6
Kiangsu	(5)	11.4
Hupeh	(5)	11.4
Shansi	(3)	6.8
Fukien	(3)	6.8
Kiangsi	(2)	4.6
Anhwei	(1)	2.3
Kwangtung	(1)	2.3
Kwangsi	(1)	2.3
Kweichow	(1)	2.3
Heilungkiang	(1)	2.3
Manchuria	(1)	2.3
Shantung	(1)	2.3
Shensi	(1)	2.3

Long March

Yes	24
No	12
Don't know	8

TABLE 3. FATHER'S STATUS: KUOMINTANG CENTRAL EXECUTIVE COMMITTEEMEN

	1924		1926		1929		1931	
	No.	Percent	No.	Percent	No.	Percent	No.	Percent
Landlord								
Scholar	—	—	(2)	5.6	—	—	—	—
Large	(3)	12.5	(3)	8.3	(4)	11.1	(2)	5.6
Medium	(3)	12.5	(3)	8.3	(1)	2.8	(2)	5.6
Small	(1)	4.2	(1)	2.8	—	—	—	—
		29.2		25.0		13.9		11.1
Merchant								
Scholar	(2)	8.3	(1)	2.8	(1)	2.8	(1)	2.8
Large	(1)	4.2	(4)	11.1	(3)	8.3	(4)	11.1
Medium	(1)	4.2	(5)	13.9	(5)	13.9	(4)	11.1
Small	(1)	4.2	(1)	2.8	(5)	13.9	(5)	13.9
		20.8		30.5		38.9		38.9
Peasant								
Large landed	—		—		—		—	
Medium landed	—		(1)	2.8	—		—	
Small landed	—		—		(1)	2.8	(1)	2.8
Landless	—		—		(1)	2.8	—	
		0.0		2.8		5.6		2.8
Scholar	(2)	8.3	(2)	5.6	—		—	
Scholar-official	(2)	8.3	(2)	5.6	(2)	5.6	(2)	5.6
Artisan								
Laborer								
Military officer								
Other—professional revolutionary	—		(2)	5.6	(1)	2.8	(1)	2.8
Don't know	(8)	33.3	(9)	25.0	(12)	33.3	(14)	38.9
		100.0		100.0		100.0		100.0
All scholars	(6)	25.0	(7)	19.4	(3)	8.3	(3)	8.3

TABLE 4. BIRTHPLACES OF CENTRAL EXECUTIVE COMMITTEEMEN

1924			1926			1929		
	No.	Percent		No.	Percent		No.	Percent
Kwangtung	(4)	16.7	Kwangtung	(7)	19.4	Kwangtung	(9)	25.0
Hupeh	(4)	16.7	Hunan	(3)	8.3	Chekiang	(6)	16.7
Hunan	(2)	8.3	Hupeh	(3)	8.3	Kiangsu	(4)	11.1
Szechwan	(2)	8.3	Chekiang	(2)	5.6	Kiangsi	(3)	8.3
Chahar	(2)	8.3	Kiangsu	(2)	5.6	Szechwan	(2)	5.6
Chekiang	(1)	4.2	Szechwan	(2)	5.6	Anhwei	(2)	5.6
Kiangsu	(1)	4.2	Kiangsi	(2)	5.6	Shansi	(2)	5.6
Kiangsi	(1)	4.2	Hopeh	(2)	5.6	Hupeh	(2)	5.6
Hopeh	(1)	4.2	Kwangsi	(2)	5.6	Hunan	(1)	2.8
Anhwei	(1)	4.2	Shensi	(2)	5.6	Kweichow	(1)	2.8
Shantung	(1)	4.2	Chahar	(1)	2.8	Shantung	(1)	2.8
Shensi	(1)	4.2	Anhwei	(1)	2.8	Shensi	(1)	2.8
Fukien	(1)	4.2	Shantung	(1)	2.8	Fukien	(1)	2.8
			Yunnan	(1)	2.8	Yunnan	(1)	2.8
Don't know	(2)	8.3	Trinidad	(1)	2.8	Don't know	(0)	—
			Siam	(1)	2.8			
			Don't know	(3)	8.3			

1931			1935			1945		
	No.	Percent		No.	Percent		No.	Percent
Kwangtung	(9)	25.0	Kwangtung	(23)	19.3	Kwangtung	(32)	14.4
Chekiang	(7)	19.4	Chekiang	(14)	11.8	Chekiang	(31)	13.9
Kiangsu	(4)	11.4	Kiangsu	(9)	7.6	Kiangsu	(24)	10.8
Kiangsi	(3)	8.3	Hupeh	(9)	7.6	Hunan	(19)	8.5
Fukien	(3)	8.3	Hunan	(7)	5.9	Szechwan	(14)	6.3
Szechwan	(2)	5.6	Kweichow	(6)	5.0	Hopeh	(11)	4.9
Hupeh	(2)	5.6	Kiangsi	(6)	5.0	Kiangsi	(11)	4.9
Kweichow	(2)	5.6	Szechwan	(5)	4.2	Anhwei	(9)	4.0
Shansi	(1)	2.8	Anhwei	(5)	4.2	Kwangsi	(8)	3.6
Shantung	(1)	2.8	Shansi	(5)	4.2	Kweichow	(8)	3.6
Shensi	(1)	2.8	Hopeh	(4)	3.4	Shansi	(8)	3.6
Yunnan	(1)	2.8	Shensi	(4)	3.4	Shantung	(7)	3.1
			Kwangsi	(3)	2.5	Hupeh	(7)	3.1
Don't know	(0)	—	Fukien	(3)	2.5	Shensi	(6)	2.7
			Yunnan	(3)	2.5	Fukien	(5)	2.2
			Liaoning	(2)	1.7	Liaoning	(4)	1.8
			Tibet	(2)	1.7	Kansu	(4)	1.8
			Shantung	(2)	1.7	Yunnan	(4)	1.8
			Kansu	(1)	.8	Tibet	(2)	.9
			Sinkiang	(1)	.8	Sinkiang	(1)	.5
			Kirin	(1)	.8	Kirin	(1)	.5
			Don't know	(4)	3.4	Honan	(1)	.5
						Suiyuan	(1)	.5
						Heilungkiang	(1)	.5
						Inner Mongolia	(1)	.5
						Honolulu	(1)	.5
						Don't know	(2)	.9

TABLE 5. EDUCATION OF CENTRAL EXECUTIVE COMMITTEEMEN

	1924		1926		1929		1931		1935		1945	
	No.	Percent	No.	Percent	No.	Percent	No.	Percent	No.	Percent	No.	Percent
Japanese university	(9)	37.5	(10)	27.8	(8)	22.2	(8)	22.2	(18)	15.1	(30)	13.5
Japanese military	(3)	12.5	(4)	11.1	(9)	25.0	(7)	19.4	(17)	14.3	(18)	8.1
Chinese university	(6)	25.0	(11)	30.6	(7)	19.4	(8)	22.2	(28)	23.5	(76)	34.1
Chinese military	(2)	8.3	(6)	16.7	(12)	33.3	(11)	30.6	(43)	36.1	(78)	35.0
Chinese classical	(6)	25.0	(5)	13.9	(7)	19.4	(4)	11.1	(11)	9.2	(8)	3.6
China only	(5)	20.8	(9)	25.0	(10)	27.8	(9)	25.0	(54)	45.4	(106)	47.5
United States	(1)	4.2	(5)	13.9	(7)	19.4	(9)	25.0	(13)	10.9	(34)	15.3
France	(3)	12.5	(2)	5.6	(1)	2.8	(—)		(3)	2.5	(9)	4.0
Germany	(1)	4.2	(1)	2.8	(1)	2.8	(1)	2.8	(4)	3.4	(13)	5.8
Great Britain	(2)	8.3	(3)	8.3	(3)	8.3	(3)	8.3	(4)	3.4	(11)	4.9
Belgium	(1)	4.2	(—)		(—)		(—)		(2)	1.7	(1)	0.5
Soviet Union	(—)		(2)	5.6	(—)		(—)		(3)	2.5	(11)	4.9
Other	(—)		(—)		(—)		(—)		(1)	0.8	(3)	1.4
None	(—)		(—)		(—)		(—)		(1)	0.8	(1)	0.5
Don't know	(4)	16.7	(6)	16.7	(—)		(1)	2.8	(9)	7.6	(9)	4.0
Total military	(4)	16.7	(7)	19.4	(14)	38.9	(12)	33.3	(51)	42.9	(87)	39.0

NOTES

1. Richard Wilhelm, <u>A Short History of Chinese Civilization</u>, translated by Joan Joshua (New York: Viking Press, 1929), pp. 215, 240, 258.

2. Karl August Wittfogel, <u>New Light on Chinese Society</u> (New York: International Secretariat, Institute of Pacific Relations, 1938), pp. 11–12.

3. E. A. Kracke, Jr., "Family vs. Merit in Chinese Civil Service Examinations under the Empire," <u>Harvard Journal of Asiatic Studies</u>, X (1947), 103–23. Cf. Karl A. Wittfogel, "Public Office in the Liao Dynasty and the Chinese Examination System," <u>op. cit.</u>, pp. 13–40.

4. Arthur W. Hummel (ed.), <u>Eminent Chinese of the Ch'ing Period</u> (2 vols.; Washington, D.C.: Government Printing Office, 1943). These twenty-three, as selected by the author for illustrative purposes, are: Chang Chih-tung, Chang Yin-huan, Jung Hung, Kuang-hsü, Tuan-fang, Li Wen-t'ien, Liu K'un-i, Yuan Shih-k'ai, Prince Ch'un, I-hsin, Feng Tzu-ts'ai, Tz'u-hsi, T'ang Chiung, Sun Chia-nai, Wu Ta-ch'eng, Jung-lu, Li Lien-ying, Sung Ch'ing, Hsü Ching-ch'eng, Liu K'un-i, Chih-jui, Ch'iu Feng-chia, T'an Ssu-t'ung.

5. The sons of two merchants advanced through the examination system, obtained <u>chin shih</u> degrees, and served for brief periods at Hanlin Academy, the highest institution of learning within the Empire.

6. For a concise account of events during this period, consult Harley Farnsworth MacNair, <u>China in Revolution</u> (Chicago: University of Chicago Press, 1931), pp. 34–64.

7. The rough outlines of this controversy can be pieced together from <u>The Communist International, Executive Committee: The Second Congress</u> (no place, no date), pp. 108–58, 475–79, 570–79, and from <u>The Second Congress of the Communist International: As Reported and Interpreted by the Official Newspapers of Soviet Russia</u> (Washington, D.C.: Government Printing Office, 1920), pp. 38–46. For the interpretation presented in this paper, the author has given considerable weight to a statement given him by M. N. Roy in Dehra Dun, India, October 15, 1950.

8. <u>Protokoll des IV Kongresses der Kommunistischen Internationale</u> (Hamburg, 1923), p. 615.

9. Ch'ien Tuan-sheng, <u>The Government and Politics of China</u> (Cambridge, 1950), pp. 119, 120, 124. See also Min-ch'ien T. Z. Tyau, <u>Two Years of Nationalist China</u> (Shanghai, 1930), p. 26. The Kuomintang Constitution appears in Arthur N. Holcombe, <u>The Chinese Revolution</u> (Cambridge: Harvard University Press, 1930), Appendix C, pp. 356–70.

10. <u>The China Year Book</u>, 1931 (Peking and Tientsin, 1931), p. 556.

11. Chih-fang Wu (W. F. Wu), <u>Chinese Government and Politics</u> (Shanghai, 1935), p. 286.

12. There is some confusion in regard to the precise Communist membership of this committee. All sources agree that T'an P'ing-shan and Yu Shu-te had seats, but it cannot be stated for certain whether or not Li Ta-chao and Kan Shu-te were also members. If they were, then their names must have been eliminated from lists published after the Kuomintang-Communist break in 1927.

13. "Protest of the Chungkuo Kuomintang Tungchi Club," <u>The China Year Book</u>, 1928, p. 1329.

14. Holcombe, <u>op. cit.</u>, p. 229.

15. For differing viewpoints in regard to this complex struggle for power, consult Harold R. Isaacs, <u>The Tragedy of the Chinese Revolution</u> (Stanford, Calif.: Stanford University Press, 1951), pp. 74–252; T'ang Leang-li, <u>The Inner History</u>

of the Chinese Revolution (London, 1930), pp. 242–44; Louis Fischer, The Soviets in World Affairs (New York: J. Cape & H. Smith, 1930) XI, 652; T. C. Woo, The Kuomintang and the Future of the Chinese Revolution (London, 1928), pp. 167–74; George Sokolsky, The Tinder Box in Asia (Garden City, N.Y.: Doubleday, Doran & Co. Inc., 1933) and The China Year Book, 1928, p. 1326.

16. Yen Hsi-shan's telegram to Chiang Kai-shek, February 24, 1931, as reprinted in The China Year Book, 1931, p. 556.

17. T. A. Bisson, "The Years of the Kuomintang: Revolution vs. Reaction," Foreign Policy Reports, VIII, No. 25 (February 15, 1933), 301.

18. Sun Fo's telegram of resignation, The China Year Book, 1934, p. 348.

19. China Weekly Review (Shanghai), February 20, 1937, p. 408.

20. Wang died of diabetes in a Japanese hospital November 10, 1944; Chou died of a heart attack in a Chinese prison in February 1948; and Ch'en was executed for treason in June 1946. For a discussion of Wang and his motives see Travers E. Durkee, "Wang Ching-wei and Japan, 1937–1940" (Master's thesis, Stanford University, 1949).

21. China Hand Book, 1937–1945 (Rev. ed.; New York: Chinese Ministry of Information, 1947), p. 96. See also Ch'ien Tuan-sheng, op. cit., p. 122.

22. Act of the Legislative Yuan, April 31, XXVI (1937), governing the election of representatives to the National Congress. Paul M. Linebarger, The China of Chiang Kai-shek (Boston: World Peace Foundation, 1941), Appendix G, p. 302.

23. Ibid., Appendix II-B, pp. 331–40.

24. Ibid., p. 141; Appendix II-B, p. 339; and Appendix II-D, p. 354.

25. The growth of cliques and their place in this balance is ably discussed by Ch'ien Tuan-sheng, op. cit., pp. 128–32.

26. Kanichi Hatano, "History of the Chinese Communist Party," Asia Mondai Koza, Vol. II (Tokyo, 1938).

27. Chung-kuo hsien-tai ko-ming yun-tung Shih ["A History of the Contemporary Revolutionary Movement in China"] (4th ed.; no place, 1938) Vol. I, chap. 5, sec. 2; Kanichi-Hatano, Gendai Shina no Seiji to Jimbutsu (Tokyo, 1937), from notes taken by John Paasche.

28. Kisselev, "A History of Communism in China," The China Illustrated Review, January 28, 1928, p. 16.

29. Ibid.

30. Ibid.

31. Chung-kuo hsien-tai ko-ming yun-tung Shih, op. cit.; South China Morning Post, February 3, 1928. Translation of a document by Chang Kuo-t'ao, seized in the Soviet Consulate in Canton in December 1927; The Second Congress of the Communist International (Moscow, 1920), p. 571.

32. "The Organization of Factory Nuclei and Fractions," International Press Correspondence (Vienna, London), February 27, 1924, pp. 111–14.

33. "Statutes of the Comintern," International Press Correspondence, June 5, 1924, p. 321.

34. Benjamin I. Schwartz, "Ch'en Tu-hsiu: Pre-Communist Phase," in "Papers on China," Vol. II, from the Regional Studies Seminars (mimeographed for private distribution by the Committee on International and Regional Studies, Harvard University, May 1948), pp. 167–97.

35. Hatano, loc. cit. For a contrary statement in regard to Ch'en's viewpoint at this time, consult Harold R. Isaacs, op. cit., p. 58.

36. "The Manifesto of the Third Congress," (mimeographed for distribution by the Russian Research Center, Harvard University, 1950.) For the position which

Borodin held, see Great Britain, Foreign Office, Russia No. 2 (1927), Documents Illustrating the Hostile Activities of the Soviet Union and the Third International Against Great Britain (London, 1927). The Soviet Union protested that these documents were forgeries, but the indications concerning Borodin's position are entirely in line with other historical evidence.

37. N. Popov, Outline History of the Communist Party of the Soviet Union, Part II (New York: International Publishers, 1934), pp. 271–73; International Press Correspondence, January 27, 1926, p. 130; Harold R. Isaacs, op. cit.; and J. Stalin, Marxism and the National and Colonial Question (New York: International Publishers, 1935), present the two viewpoints.

38. "Letter from Shanghai," in Leon Trotsky, Problems of the Chinese Revolution (New York: Pioneer Publishers, 1932) present the two viewpoints.

39. Jay Calvin Huston in a dispatch circa spring 1928 entitled, "Sun Yat-sen, the Kuomintang, and the Chinese Russian Political Economic Alliance" (Huston Collection in the Hoover Library, Stanford, Calif.), p. 126, quotes a letter from Chief of the Russian Military Group Kissanka to Karakhan. This letter is one of many documents purportedly seized in a Chinese raid on the Soviet Embassy in Peking in April 1927.

40. Ibid., p. 127. Huston quotes a report from Soviet agent Stepanoff to his superiors in Peking. This is another document purportedly captured in the Peking raid.

41. Isaacs, op. cit., p. 84; cf. T'ang, op. cit., pp. 234–47.

42. Huston, "Sun Yat-sen, the Kuomintang, and the Chinese Russian Political Economic Alliance," op. cit., pp. 134–39.

43. The resolutions limiting Communist activities appear in T. C. Woo, op. cit., pp. 175–77.

44. Report on the Activity of the Communist International March—November 1926 (no place, no date), p. 119.

45. International Press Correspondence, March 31, 1927, p. 446.

46. Pravda, March 16, 1927.

47. Pravda, April 15, 1927.

48. International Press Correspondence, June 16, 1927, pp. 731–41.

49. Ch'en Tu-hsiu, "Political and Organizational Report of the Central Committee," International Press Correspondence, June 9, 1927, pp. 716–17.

50. "Manifesto of the August 7 Conference of the Chinese Communist Party, August 7, 1927," and files of the People's Tribune, Hankow, for May 1927.

51. J. Stalin, op. cit., p. 249.

52. According to one source, Wang Ching-wei, returning to China in the spring of 1927 on the advice of the Russians, had stopped over in Moscow long enough to agree to a program which included land confiscation and other points urged by Stalin. But Wang, influenced by such "known reactionaries" as Sun Fo, Eugene Chen, and T'an Yen-k'ai, who had "come to a secret understanding with Chiang Kai-shek," was no longer in a position to accept Stalin's advice—M. N. Roy, Revolution and Counter-Revolution in China (Calcutta, 1946), p. 519. It is entirely possible that Wang did agree to a general program without comprehending its full implications. The rest of this assertion is open to question.

53. P. Mif, Heroic China: Fifteen Years of the Communist Party of China (New York: Worker's Library Publishers, 1937), p. 53.

54. Stalin, as reported in Pravda, July 28, 1927, "A Resolution on the International Situation," International Press Correspondence, August 18, 1927, p 1076.

55. International Press Correspondence, August 4, 1927, p. 1006.

56. The Communist International: Between the Fifth and Sixth World Congresses, 1924–28 (London, 1928), pp. 451–52.

57. Edgar Snow, Red Star Over China, (Rev. ed.; New York: Garden City Publishing Co., 1939), p. 149.

58. The office of Secretary General never regained the prestige lost when Ch'en Tu-hsiu was deposed.

59. Chinese Communist Party Yearbook (Japanese Foreign Ministry, 1935).

60. Mif, op. cit., p. 54. Listed as members of the "Revolutionary Committee" for the Nanchang Uprising were such Kuomintang leftists as Mme. Sun Yat-sen, Teng Yen-ta, and Eugene Chen, en route to European exile at the time, and General Chang Fa-kuei, who soon displayed remarkable efficiency at exterminating Communists.

61. Ibid.

62. Pravda, September 30, 1927.

63. Mif, op. cit., p. 55.

64. A. Neuberg (Heinz Neumann), L'Insurrection Armée (Paris, 1931); International Press Correspondence, December 12, 1928, p. 1672.

65. "Theses and Resolutions of the VI World Congress of the Communist International," International Press Correspondence, December 12, 1928, p. 1672.

66. "A Letter to the Central Committee of the Chinese Communist Party from the Executive Committee of the Comintern (approved by the Political Secretariat of the Comintern, October 26, 1929)," Hung Ch'i ["Red Flag"], No. 76, February 15, 1930.

67. "Molotov's Report to the Sixteenth Congress of the Communist Party of the Soviet Union," Vsesoiuznaia kommunisticheskaia partiia (bol'shevikov): XVI S"ezd Vsesoiuznoi kommunisticheskoi partii, Stenograficheskii otchet (Moscow, 1931), pp. 415–16.

68. Report on the Activity of the Communist International, March–November, 1926, p. 118.

69. "Letter from the Central Committee of the Chinese Communist Party to all Party members," Hung Ch'i, No. 87, March 26, 1930.

70. "Notice of the Central Committee of the Chinese Communist Party," Hung Ch'i, February 15, 1930.

71. Chou En-lai, Report to the Third Plenum (no place, no date). Chou En-lai seems to have escaped the severe criticism suffered by Ch'iu. To date, the record of Chou's relationships with various leadership cliques and with Moscow is in need of clarification.

72. "The Report of the Oriental Department of the Comintern," Pu-erh-sai-wei-ko (Bolshevik), May 10, 1931. This issue contains various materials pertaining to Li Li-san's "trial in Moscow."

73. "The Discussion of the Li Li-san Line by the Presidium of the Executive Committee of the Communist International," and Manuilsky's statement, ibid.

74. Mao Tse-tung, "Report on an Investigation of the Peasant Movement in Hunan" (translated and mimeographed for private distribution by the Russian Research Center, Harvard University, 1950.)

75. Compare Mif, op. cit., p. 68, with Anna Louise Strong, "The Thought of Mao Tse-tung," Amerasia, June 1947, p. 166. Mao's relationship to the "pure proletarian line" at the time is a matter for investigation. According to Ypsilon, Pattern for World Revolution (New York: Ziff-Davis Publishing Co, 1947), p. 425, Mao was called to Moscow for instructions on at least two occasions (1931 and 1934), but convincing evidence of these journeys has yet to be presented.

76. Mao actually, if not officially, had long since set up a rural soviet system, but Moscow had continued to think in urban terms.

77. International Press Correspondence, June 10, 1931, p. 552.

78. Räte-China, Documente der Chinesichen Revolution (Moscow-Leningrad, 1934); International Press Correspondence, January 23, 1933, p. 91.

79. Chang Kuo-t'ao in an interview with the author, Hong Kong, November 3, 1950.

80. O. Briere, "The Twenty-five Years of the Chinese Communist Party, 1921–1946," Aurora University Bulletin, VII, No. 3 (1946), 111. There is some doubt concerning the exact date of the Central Committee's transfer to Juichin and about the relationship, at this time, between the Chinese Communist Party and Chinese Soviet power. Presumably Mao increased his power through his position in the Central Soviet. But it is not clear whether or not Mif's protégés had already lost their influence, nor is it certain whether Mao received Moscow's instructions directly or through Central Committee headquarters. There is also some question whether the "returned students" associated themselves with Mao voluntarily, through direction from Moscow, or by force of circumstances alone. Chang Kuo-t'ao expressed the opinion to the author that Mao's position was relatively unimportant until the Tsun-yi Conference and that all directives passed through regular channels.

81. Accounts of Red Army actions against the Kuomintang are available in Snow, op. cit., pp. 157–67; Nym Wales, Inside Red China (New York: Doubleday, Doran & Co., 1939), pp. 251–56; Victor A. Yakhontov, The Chinese Soviets (New York: Coward-McCann, Inc., 1934), pp. 100–21. There are also numerous scattered articles in the files of International Press Correspondence.

82. Chang interview.

83. "Report of Mao Tse-tung to the Second Congress of Chinese Soviets," International Press Correspondence, June 29, 1934, p. 957; July 6, 1934, p. 977.

84. Chang interview.

85. Briere, loc. cit. See also Susumu Kinoshita, The Chinese Communist Party and Its Politics (Tokyo, 1948).

86. International Press Correspondence, January 26, 1933, p. 91.

87. Shigeo Watanabe, Sho Kaiseki to Mo Shitaku ["Chiang Kai-shek and Mao Tse-tung"], (Tokyo, 1941), Harvard-Yenching Library. Cited by Chao Kuo-chun, "Thirty Years of the Communist Movement in China" (Russian Research Center, Harvard University, 1950); International Press Correspondence, December 21, 1935, p. 1728.

88. International Press Correspondence, August 20, 1935, pp. 971–72.

89. Ibid., November 9, 1935, p. 1489.

90. Chang interview.

91. International Press Correspondence, December 2, 1935, p. 1666.

92. Chang interview.

93. International Press Correspondence, September 19, 1935, p. 1181.

94. Mao Tse-tung and others, China, The March Toward Unity (New York: Workers' Library, 1937), pp. 119–23, gives Communist releases concerning the Sian incident.

95. "Communist Statement on Unity (1937)." For an English translation, see Lawrence K. Rosinger, China's Wartime Politics 1937–1944 (Princeton: Princeton University Press, 1944), pp. 96–97.

96. Chang interview.

97. Communist International, XV, No. 7 (July, 1938), 688–89.

98. The differences between junior cadres who had been working in front line areas and those who had remained in various Party headquarters has been noted by Michael Lindsay, "Post War Government and Politics of Communist China," Post War Governments of the Far East (Gainesville, Fla.: University of Florida, 1947).

99. Mao Tse-tung, China's New Democracy. An English translation is available in U. S. Congress, House Foreign Affairs Committee Report, Strategy and Tactics of World Communism, Supplement No. C, Appendix (Washington, D.C.: U.S. Government Printing Office, 1948), p. 75.

100. For Party reform documents pertaining to this development, see Mao's China, with translation and introduction by Boyd Compton (Seattle, Wash.: University of Washington Press, 1952.).

101. U. S. Congress, House Foreign Affairs Committee, National and International Movements. Report: The Strategy and Tactics of World Communism. Supplement IV, p. iii.

102. Kao Kang's report has been translated and mimeographed by the American Consulate General, Hong Kong, Current Background, No. 163, March 5, 1952.

103. Fei Hsiao-tung and Chang Chih-i, Earthbound China (Chicago: University of Chicago Press, 1945), p. 277, cited in Morton H. Fried, "Military Status in Chinese Society," American Journal of Sociology, LVII, No. 4 (1952), 349–50.

104. "New China News Agency in English Morse to North America, December 19, 1949."

105. The relative importance of Russian-supplied Japanese arms, and arms captured from Japanese and Kuomintang troops by the Chinese Communists themselves, is a subject of controversy which is not likely to be settled except through the perspective of history.

106. According to the People's Hand Book (Hong Kong, 1950), Section F, p. 7, this party was organized by Chinese in the United States in 1925. During a conference in Hong Kong, May 1, 1947, the group adopted a platform calling for peace and political democracy and opposing dictatorship by a single party.

107. These posts include the State Administrative Council officers, members, and Secretariat, as well as the heads and vice-heads of the 21 Portfolio Ministries, the four Committees, the three Commissions, the four Administrations, the Academy of Science, and the People's Bank.

108. American Consulate General, Hong Kong, Current Background, No. 170, April 8, 1952.

spoke joe to jack

leave her alone
she's not your gal

jack spoke to joe
's left crashed
pal dropped

o god alice
yells but who shot
up grabbing had
by my throat me

give it him good
a bottle she
quick who stop damned
fall all we go spill

and chairs tables the and
bitch whispers jill
mopping too bad

dear sh not yet
jesus what blood

darling i said

red-rag and pink-flag
blackshirt and brown
strut-mince and stink-brag
have all come to town

some like it shot
and some like it hung
and some like it in the two·
nine months young